No Continuing City

No Continuing City

GENERAL FREDERICK COUTTS, C.B.E.

*'Not as though I had already attained,
either were made perfect . . .'*

SALVATIONIST PUBLISHING AND SUPPLIES, LTD.,
JUDD STREET, KING'S CROSS, LONDON WC1H 9NN

©Copyright The Salvation Army 1978

First published 1976
by Hodder and Stoughton Limited

Paperback edition 1978
by Salvationist Publishing and Supplies, Limited,
Judd Street, King's Cross,
London WC1H 9NN

ISBN 0 85412 327 X

Contents

NOTE: The ranks given to Salvationists in these pages are those held at the time of reference.

Contents

I

Know Thou the God of Thy Fathers

As a matter of routine the Registrar for the district of Dysart noted that a boy named Frederick had been born to John and Mary Coutts of Park Road, West Gallatown, at 2.15 p.m. on September 21st, 1899. But Thursday's child had far to go, and Kirkcaldy was not to be his continuing city for long. Within less than two months he and his parents had crossed the Firth of Forth to Penicuik. It was therefore hardly by virtue of any residential qualification that sixty-six years later, on Monday, May 31st, 1965, the Royal Burgh admitted him as a 'guild brother, burgess and freeman'—the tenth name to be added to the roll since that of William Booth on April 16th, 1906.

This first change was only the beginning of his many wanderings. At the age of eight months he found himself in another new home in Murieston Terrace, Edinburgh; at fourteen months in Bethcar Terrace, Ebbw Vale; at two years and two months in 30, Vauxhall Road, Gloucester. Thereafter similar moves followed at annual intervals or less. Four months before his third birthday he was taken to 77, Gloucester Road, Trowbridge; twelve months later to Gold Croft, Yeovil, where on August 22nd, 1903, he was joined by another brother, Ernest, though within less than two months they both were taken to new quarters at 13, Clifton Terrace, Barnstaple. The next ten years saw the two boys living at 45, Cameron Street, Cardiff; 69, Regent Street, Bristol; 10, Orchard Street, Street; 22, Shakespeare Street, Loughborough; 152, Boundary Road,

St. Helens; 5, Walker Street, Warrington; 164, Great Junction Street, Leith and 52, Helenvale Street, Parkhead, Glasgow. Those who have read thus far may have realised that their parents were corps officers in The Salvation Army, and their itinerant life was part of the legacy of Methodism inherited by William and Catherine Booth and embodied in the administrative structure of the Movement which they founded in 1865.

In the following year John Coutts was born of poor parents a few miles outside of Aberdeen and, early wearying of the monotony of village life, stole away from home before he was thirteen years of age to find work in Dundee as a half-timer. After eighteen months he returned to Aberdeen to continue working in the shipyard and to discover The Salvation Army installed in the St. Katherine's Hall in the city.

The lad made up his mind to see these new soldiers and, nothing if not persistent, managed to evade the hallkeeper on guard at the door. Once inside, he found himself one of a congregation of eleven hundred people. He was not ignorant of the Scriptures. In his time he had attended as many as three Sunday-schools on the one Presbyterian Sabbath. But this was a presentation of the Christian faith very different from the sober worship of the village kirk. The Captain paced up and down the platform in his shirt sleeves. The bonnets the women wore were almost as large as his mother's coal scuttle. The men wore guernseys, much the same as the fishermen at the docks, only crimson in colour and embroidered with various legends he did not wholly understand. There was an atmosphere of reverent irreverence about the place, but two things were plain. The Captain and his comrades were undeniably happy and unmistakably in earnest.

When an invitation was given to the Mercy Seat, the newcomer went forward but, as this was speedily filled, no one spoke to him save a kindly grey-haired man who asked him 'if he believed'. The lad said that he did and, uninvited, turned up on the following Sunday at the evening open-air meeting. No one spoke to him but, nothing daunted, he took his place in the march and found himself facing the hallkeeper

once more. 'I joined', he earnestly explained, 'last Sunday'—
but even then only with reluctance did the guardian of law and
order let him in.

Sadly the new convert fell ill, spent four weeks in hospital,
and altogether nearly three months elapsed before he was able
to attend another meeting. No one enquired about him, and
the comrades wrote him off as a backslider—one in whom the
seed had quickly sprung up but equally quickly had withered.
At his first appearance the zealous Captain was for dragging
him to the Mercy Seat again, there to repent of his fall from
grace. But the presumed prodigal protested that he had only
fallen ill, whereupon it began to dawn upon the officer that
it was he who should repent—of his failure to shepherd one
of his sheep.

The lad had need of his native doggedness for, when his
family heard that he was thinking of officership, they wrote to
the Army authorities to warn them that he was dying of con-
sumption and, to put his undone condition beyond doubt, to
William Booth to say that he was out of his mind. But on
November 14th, 1887, he was accepted as a candidate for
officership and bidden by one, Thomas Cumberbeach, to
bring with him £1 for his uniform. Should he lack this sum,
he was authorised to collect it. Three weeks later he was
directed to present himself at the Salvation Army training
depot in New Street, St. Neots, Huntingdonshire—which he
did by sailing from Aberdeen to London, then the thriftiest
way of covering the five hundred miles.

On March 1st, 1888—that is, after little more than ten
weeks of 'training'—he was appointed a Cadet-Captain to
Stotfold and, four months later, a fully fledged Captain without
qualifying prefix to Swanage. Thereafter he commanded the
corps at Shifnal, Potton, Milford Haven, Pembroke Dock,
Haverfordwest, Glastonbury, Elgin, Kirkwall, Leslie, Tilli-
coultry, Forfar, St. Andrews, Stirling, Broughty Ferry,
Buckhaven and Perth—in that order, receiving at the last-
named an official wedding grant of £3.

Meanwhile a Welsh girl named Mary Jones had entered the
training depot at Walthamstow and, on June 2nd, 1891, was

appointed to the 665th corps at Cardigan. She welcomed the appointment. This was her homeland. Welsh was her native tongue. She read her Bible in Welsh. She said her prayers in Welsh, a habit she never lost. From Cardigan she want to Neyland, to Penclwdd, to Pwllheli, to Conway, to Dolgelly, to Bangor, to Llanwrst, to Llanfairfechan, to Blaenau Ffestiniog, to Bethesda, to Ruthin, to Higham, to Conisborough, to Bolsover, to Gilfach Goch, to Newry and finally to Belfast. The ways of John and Mary must have crossed when, on December 3rd, 1891, they found themselves at the nearby corps of Milford Haven and Neyland respectively, though it was not until October 24th, 1898, that they were married. No hurried, fly-by-night affairs were permitted by the Salvation Army discipline of that day. The contracting parties had to be sure that they knew their own mind, and distance, not to mention time, was held to be an infallible test.

By the time John and Mary had become officers the decade of the physical persecution of Salvationists was virtually over. As against the lethargy (at the best) or the prejudice (at the worst) of certain mayors and chief constables, the Home Secretary had ruled that Salvationists should be given all needful protection upon their lawful occasions—which included religious processioning. But public brutality was not the deadliest foe. Defying visible opposition could arouse a certain elation of spirit, but there was little uplift in the constant struggle to keep body and soul together on short commons. Daily fortitude was needed to live, as John did at Shifnal on seven shillings and one penny a week, or at Kirkwall on eight shillings and three halfpence a week, or at Milford Haven on six shillings and sevenpence a week. He must have felt that manna was falling from heaven when at St. Andrews he received sixteen shillings and threepence a week and, newly married at Kirkcaldy, he and his bride must have counted themselves passing rich on £70 a year. Not that their allowances were ever much over £100 a year even up to the middle of the First World War. In 1916 the full weekly allowance for officers of their rank, with two children still at school, was £2 1s. 6d. weekly, plus furnished quarters. Should any student of

religious affairs wish to enquire how the work of The Salvation
Army in Great Britain was steadfastly maintained until
upborne on a wave of public popularity evoked by public
service during two world wars, he should not overlook the
uncomplaining willingness of many officers to live on a shoe-
string for the sake of the cause.

Not that we two boys were unhappy on account of this. Far
from it. Our parents did not off-load their burdens on to our
shoulders. The continual change of town—and therefore of
schools—had its drawbacks (of which more anon) but for us
it also had its thrills. Columbus was not more elated on sighting
the new world than we were to explore the new quarters where
we were to live. Would there be two single beds in our bedroom, or was it—as usual—one double bed between us? We
knew almost in advance that the sofa in the front room would
be the customary horsehair. Three-piece suites were unheard
of. Nevertheless upstairs, downstairs, in my lady's chamber
we wandered, eager to discover any new delights—if thus they
could be described. I can still recall the excitement of coming
to a house with a bathroom. That was in 1909—but such was
the rare exception rather than the rule. It was 1930 before I
enjoyed similar mod. cons. for myself and my young family.

The stately homes of our boyhood included a terraced
house in Bootle; a country cottage in Somerset; a first-floor
tenement flat in Glasgow with a bed in the kitchen recess and
another in the front room. In that particular setting economy
of space was as much a necessity as a virtue. Opposite the
black-leaded kitchen range, boasting an oven on the one side
and a hot water boiler, complete with polished brass tap, on
the other, was a box-like arrangement whose lid carried any
spare kitchen-ware but which had to be lifted when the coal-
man called. Blessed was he among men who raised the least
amount of coal dust as he emptied the contents of his bag into
the wooden bunker. But even the most dexterous of his tribe
was not overly welcome if, during a wet spell, the family
washing was still hanging damply from the clothes rack which
was operated by a pulley attached to the kitchen wall. The
art of pouring a quart into a pint pot achieved its final triumph

when a couple of stout hooks, firmly secured in the bathroom
ceiling, provided a space where a bicycle might be hung. In
such a setting the most rumbustious youngster had to adopt
what it is now fashionable to describe as 'a low profile'. The
measured rapping of a broomhead underneath the kitchen
floor—the ceiling of the tenant below—was warning enough
that small boys, even when not seen, were neither to be heard.

But never unwillingly to school, though some experiences
in the field of learning were happier than others. At Loughborough in 1908 I occupied a place at a long continuous desk,
which stretched the width of the classroom, and was provided
with a slate and a slate pencil. Nothing amiss with a slate.
Magnus Magnusson has testified that the preparatory school
of the Edinburgh Academy used slates until 1912—in fact a
blessing in disguise, for a furtive spot of spit could obliterate
the stupidest mistake without teacher knowing a thing about
it. My mortification arose from the fact that the class into
which I was placed was already doing 'pounds, shillings and
pence'. This stage in my formal education had not been reached
at the country school from which I had come. No one enquired
whether I knew that twelve pence made one shilling and twenty
shillings one pound. I struggled to lighten my own darkness
without betraying my ignorance, but it was the 'carrying
forward' which proved my stone of stumbling. I slid off my
seat at the midday break to bear home my boyish humiliation.

Still, other schools had their compensations. At Warrington
I attended one which boasted the high-flown name of the
People's College where school money—a few pence each week
—was paid every Monday morning. One teacher hit on the
happy device of lining the whole class around the wall for a
kind of general knowledge bee. The brighter spirits were
placed at the lower end, but these could rise according to their
ability to reply to such questions as others had been unable to
answer. My few roving years had gained me odd bits of
knowledge which came in useful at such times.

I now see that horizons began to widen—in ways pleasant
as well as unpleasant—when my parents were given appointments first in Edinburgh and then in Glasgow. Here for the

first time I faced the taws, freely used by some—though certainly not all—masters in the cause of learning. But it seemed to one boy less barbarous than the thick rounded ruler employed south of the border which could descend with numbing force upon one's open palm. The taws stung more, but on the way from one's seat to the front of the class—for discipline of this nature was always administered as publicly as possible— it was possible to shake down one's coat sleeve to cover one's wrist, and the boy with a quick eye could withdraw his hand at the moment of impact. This is known in boxing circles, so I am told, as 'riding the punch'.

Punishments aside, those years did well by me even though the curriculum included no games of any description. The one relaxation from the classroom was woodwork, but I was never very much good with my hands. 'Woody', our instructor, was kind-hearted enough to shape up my botches, and the terror of the taws began to die away as it slowly dawned on me that its use depended as much upon the teacher's temperament as my ignorance. One of our masters was interested enough to ask whether I had any thought of going on to the university. I was to let him know if he could help in any way. I mentioned this to my parents, but it was beyond their frugal means—and possibly their world as well. But they did what they could, and I can never be grateful enough to them for that.

Meanwhile my brother and I enjoyed both the Firth of Forth and the Firth of Clyde. There was the incomparable castle crowning Edinburgh which, with Arthur's Seat, provided a paradise for boys. The cable cars moved at their steady pace along Princes Street and the way in which, at the top of Leith Street and at other strategic points, the motorman birled his wheel around as he changed from one underground cable to another, never lost its fascination.

At that time one could travel by train from Edinburgh to Leith on three different routes. There was the direct line from Waverley to Leith Central, via Abbeyhill, which took but six minutes. There was a more circuitous route from Waverley to North Leith by way of Easter Road and Bonnington, with a station in Junction Road not more than a couple of hundred

yards from our first-floor flat. The most leisurely route of all
was from the Caledonian station at the western end of Princes
Street to Leith, calling at Dalry Road, Murrayfield, Craig-
leith,. Granton Road and Newhaven, a journey of nineteen
minutes for which a boy, travelling half-fare first class, paid
one penny. 'Travel by Caley' ran a station poster of the time.
On those terms we needed no second invitation. Apart from
railway warrants, officers', issued for the use of, during the First
World War, half-a-century was to pass before I enjoyed such
luxury again.

Nor was Glasgow content to take second place in the matter
of cheap and abundant transport, whether by land or sea.
For a 'haupn'y hauf' the young teenager could travel by tram—
upper deck or lower deck as his fancy pleased —from Argyle
Street to Parkhead Cross. For a shilling he could go 'doon the
watter' from the Broomielaw to Dunoon and back again. If
the journey grew tedious before the Tail o' the Bank was
reached, there was always a musicianly trio on board who
played with unflagging energy such favourites as 'The Flowers
of Edinburgh' and 'Loch Lomond', and who solicited the
practical appreciation of their captive audience with equal zeal.

To crown all there was the Army—which meant that I
had little time to kill. Sunday began at ten o'clock with the
Directory class (that is, instruction in the Army's 'catechism'),
followed at two o'clock by the company meeting (that is, the
Sunday-school class), by means of which, over a period of
years, the regular attender gained a working knowledge of the
principal Bible stories in Old and New Testament alike. There
were also adult meetings which we could attend at eleven
o'clock, at three o'clock and—our parents permitting—at a
quarter to seven. No one had to force us to go. Punishment was
to be kept away. Along with a great multitude of children like
us, we knew nothing of the alleged gloom of the Victorian
Sunday.

Membership of one of the musical sections—either young
people's or adults'—meant attendance at the weekly practices.
My mother had also set her heart on my learning to play the
piano which, in that pre-radio, pre-television and pre-cinema

age was the family instrument. Somehow—I cannot imagine how she did it—she skimped and saved enough to buy one secondhand, complete with large wooden case for transport from quarters to quarters. The packing thereof was a major labour at farewell times. Pillows and blankets were used to pad the precious instrument against the hazards of the journey. Perfection in this art was achieved if, when the front lid was finally screwed on, there was ne'er a rattle. But to practise the art I fear I had to be driven. In one of our quarters there was an ancient wall clock of which the minute hand, to my boyish imagination, moved more swiftly downwards from twelve to six than upwards from six to twelve. Hence my contrivings that compulsory attendance at the keyboard should commence at the hour rather than the half-hour, or at least by five past than twenty-five to.

My father—equally eager with my mother to keep first things first—saw no reason why I should not use my newly acquired 'skill' in the service of the Army. Those who are familiar with the part played by impromptu song and chorus in certain Army meetings will know the value of an accompanist who can 'play by ear'. I was supposed—in error, I hasten to add—to possess this gift. The truth is that I had the effrontery to play without music but also without overmuch regard for the laws of music. I am clad in sackcloth and ashes whenever I recall the wounds suffered by any sensitive hearer. I can only plead in extenuation that, learning the hard way, at least I learnt by my mistakes.

By early 1915 I was of age to join the senior band and my application to do so was signed by my father as the corps officer, and counter-signed by the bandmaster and two other senior census board members—in ecclesiastical language the elders or deacons. In reply to one of the fifteen questions on the form I stated that during the previous four weeks I had attended eighteen open-air and twenty-one indoor meetings. Musical learning may have sat lightly on us—though hardly in the sense usually intended—but what we lacked in skill we sought to make up in dedication. When this form had been approved at divisional level I was called upon to sign what was

known as a band member's bond in which, according to the
printed script, I addressed myself to 'William Bramwell Booth,
General of The Salvation Army' and declared that:

> In consideration of your appointing or considering the
> proposal to appoint me . . . to be a bandsman . . . I do
> hereby solemnly promise and engage and pledge my faith
> and loyalty, and agree and undertake with and to you or
> other the General for the time being of The Salvation
> Army . . .
>   1. To carry out the Orders and Regulations now in
> force . . .
>   2. To use any instrument or other property which may be
> entrusted to me, or which may in any way come into my
> hands, for the purposes of The Salvation Army only . . .
>   3. To deliver up, in the event of your cancelling my
> appointment or proposed appointment, to the Divisional
> Commander, the Commanding Officer of the corps, or any
> other person whom you may appoint in that behalf, any
> and all Moneys, Musical Instruments, Cases, Boxes, Stands,
> Books, Papers, or any other property of which I may have
> become possessed by virtue or in consequence of my said
> appointment.

I cannot at this time of day swear that I read all the small print,
but over a sixpenny stamp there can still be read the unsteady
signature of a boy.

The hardest thing that might be said of us was that ours was
zeal without overmuch knowledge. About this time the bandmaster decided that we should essay—a word beloved of a
future editorial colleague of mine when he wished to wound
but was afraid to strike—a selection of Salvation Army music
by Colonel F. G. Hawkes entitled 'West Indian Melodies'.
The very first bar presented us with a problem we had not
previously encountered. There was a leap from middle G (a
crotchet) to top G (a minim) ornamented by a turn and bearing
the mystic sign ♯. Without any full score (which in later years
I discovered carried the notation in full) the cornets were

bewildered, nor was the bandmaster able to enlighten them. As in the confusion at Ephesus some cried one thing and some another. After a period of trial and obvious error, it was agreed to ignore both the turn and the sharp in the sure and certain hope that few in our audiences would be any the wiser. Neither was I—at the time!

But no sentence should be written or read as if I was indifferent to the debt owed to those early tutors. At Leith Deputy-Bandmaster James Dalgleish taught my brother and me how to play a brass instrument. The horrific noises which can be produced by a beginner have to be heard to be believed. Nor can those who have never attempted to march and to play at the same time realise the difficulties which literally beset a learner's steps. The seeming ease with which present-day bandsmen move along the smooth surface of Oxford Street displays an art which conceals art. We boys raised the dust in the young people's hall at Leith as—with the seats piled up alongside the walls and in preparation for our first away engagement—we stamped our way around, trying to step off with the left foot, to cover off from front to rear, to dress by the right and to play the correct notes—all at once!

But the band was not our only interest. No boy or girl who came to the Army hall in Bangor Road between 1908 and 1920 could ever forget the diminutive young people's sergeant-major (or Sunday school superintendent). Her unflagging energy and inventive mind made up for any lack of inches. A fatal accident in the autumn of 1922 robbed the corps of James Dalgleish while he was still in his prime but 'Miss Goodlet'—as the children respectfully called her—seemed to go on for ever.

With some of the lads of that day—Alex Dewar for one—I never lost touch. He became the senior bandmaster at Leith in 1930 and was deceptively well read in the history and theology of his native land. In later years more than one Sassenach visitor who might think he had impressed his hearers by his superior erudition would be gently but effectively unhorsed by the bandmaster. It has to be admitted that a measure of guile was not wholly absent—but how was a stranger to know that an interest in brass banding could be allied to an equal interest in theology? (In later years I discovered that Colonel Arthur Goldsmith drove the same pair-in-hand. This distinguished player-composer was also a member of the Army's international doctrine council.) But to return. 'Thank you for your address, Captain' (or Major, Colonel or Commissioner, as the case might be). 'But I wondered whether you had read what John Oman wrote about your last point?' There was a riposte to this innocent form of one-upmanship but as Alex is still living, though at this time of day far frae the heath and the heather, it would be unfair to reveal it.

As at Leith so at Parkhead, where I became a senior soldier. Over the years I salute the disinterested service of 'Daddy' Long, our young people's sergeant-major, of Bandmaster James McDicken, of Treasurer John McIntyre, of Secretary Frederick Sedding (later to become a Councillor, and then Baillie, of the City of Glasgow), of the youthful Songster Leader Howard and of Corps Sergeant-Major 'Bob' Brown. Their labour in the Lord is not forgotten.

2

Deal Gently with the Young Man

THE FIRST WORLD WAR broke out while I was still in my teens
and a recruiting centre was opened in Bath Street, Glasgow,
close to the office where I was working. The 'Derby scheme'
invited the under-eighteens to attest, offering in return a
khaki brassard (which I never wore) and half-a-crown (which
imprudently I spent without delay).

Later on calling-up papers summoned me to the same
address and I presented myself before a sergeant seated at a
trestle table. For all my assumed nonchalance—or this is what
I fondly imagined it to be—I was an innocent abroad. My
somewhat sheltered existence was small preparation for life
in the armed forces. My father, in his own reserved way, was
not fully persuaded that the conflict was between St. George
and the dragon. Nor was I entirely clear why all Germans
should be regarded as Huns, lineal descendants of Attila, for
but recently German Salvationists had stayed in our home and
plainly they were no less devoted to the Christian cause than
ourselves. My dear mother prayed with me and for me—and
always continued to do so—but my immediate saviour was the
anonymous sergeant before whom I stood.

I had expected nothing better than to be posted to Gailes
where recruits for the Highland Light Infantry were doing
their square bashing. After a glance at my school record,
however, the sergeant suggested that I present myself at a
more distant table where applicants for a commission in the

19

Royal Flying Corps were being interviewed. My understandably confused account as to why I wished to join the
flying arm—for this was a totally unexpected turn of the wheel—
must have found favour for I was issued with a railway warrant
for Farnborough. Not until later did it dawn on me that by
now the authorities must have been scraping the barrel.

For the immediate future my unspoken motto was 'Sufficient
unto the day . . .'—though how dark and pervasive was that
evil was as yet hidden from my sight. At the time there seemed
to be no practical alternative to letting the chips fall where they
would. One of the service anthems of this period was: 'We're
here because we're here because . . .' (and so on ad lib.). To be
posted to X was as good—or as bad—as being posted to Y. The
going was roughish but tolerable, and to be in training as a
flying officer was a prospect into which the harsher realities of
actual warfare had not yet broken. What was also not plain
was that neither Farnborough—nor any posting thereafter—
could provide a teenager with any adequate preparation for
adult life. I see now that it could not have been expected to
do so. Maybe I lent too ready an ear to those unofficial instructors who abounded and who, by precept and practice,
were ready to advise all and sundry in the dubious arts of
dodging the column, or swinging the lead, or engaging in any
other of the manifold forms of sprucing or skiving. Maybe our
flight had more than its share of wild boys, but it hardly made
for edification when, standing easy during a break in morning
drill, the sergeant—a seconded regular—favoured his captive
audience with a blow by blow account of his encounter with
an unfortunate Asian girl for whose services he had paid in
cash. Nor have I forgotten the quiet rejoinder of another Scots
lad, standing about sixth along the line from me, when some
other N.C.O. launched into an unsolicited exposition of the
raptures and roses of vice. Not in such Swinburnian terms, of
course. But it was a wonder that the lad's name and number
was not taken on the spot!

Anyone with experience of service life will know the buzzes
and rumours which, like Jonah's gourd, spring up in a night
and perish in a night but which, during their brief life, make

compulsive listening and inspire instant—if misguided—action. A cry arose for volunteers to be trained to man captive balloons on the Western Front. A certain pricking of the thumbs, however, warned the most gullible that they might be offering themselves as sitting targets for some minor Richthofen. So that one died the death. Later on the news went round that the Royal Naval Air Service was seeking personable transfers. 'Personable!' We rose to the bait like fish to a fly. On Tusser's principle of 'naught venture, naught have', a dozen of us set down our names. We could have spared ourselves the trouble. We journeyed to Roehampton early one morning, had a whip round at Redhill (where we changed trains) so that the accompanying sergeant might renew his strength at the bar—and returned late the same evening, weighed in the balances and found wanting. Yet by some process, the details of which have been forgotten, I arrived eventually at Eastchurch on the island of Sheppey where wing and commission were secured some months later.

Here we were instructed in the elements of wireless telegraphy. In land machines and seaplanes a weighted aerial was wound around a drum and, at a safe height, the wire was paid out and carried astern in the slipstream. The process was reversed on descent and between these two points there would be two-way conversation. Schooling was also provided in aerial photography, and while there was a small square in the cockpit floor which could be removed to allow vertical pictures to be taken, most were angled views taken over the side with the camera secured by a cord around the observer's neck. It was the pilot's nightmare that some ham-fisted beginner in the seat behind him might drop the camera damaging the plane to their joint destruction.

Bombing was practised with dummy bombs and gunnery with live ammunition. At that time of day bomb sights were so primitive that little accurate allowance could be made for the strength of the wind or the crab-like drift of the plane. But carried out over the shallow waters of the Thames estuary these trial runs harmed neither man nor beast. Gunnery was more serious as we flew low over the fields of Sheppey. My pilot indicated the target area but perhaps did not notice a man who I thought was perilously near the prescribed field of fire. As this was my first practice I feared for my inaccurate aim. Fortunately (?) the gun jammed and I failed to free it, but the pilot's opinion of my fighting skills could not have been heightened by this episode.

There were less lethal exercises, as when, seated high in one of the hangars, we engaged in ship recognition as models of the German fleet were laid out in line of battle across the floor. We were told that we were to be the eyes of the fleet. One or two of us had Mittyish visions of sending the First Sea Lord some such message as: 'Eight forty-three ack emma stop Derflingger Seydlitz Molkte and Von der Tann proceeding S.S.E. at speed stop Present position estimated . . .' But for us *der tag* never dawned. By this time the R.N.A.S. and the R.F.C. had been united as the Royal Air Force, and half-a-dozen of us were posted to Mudros, just off the entrance to the Dardanelles. Ours not to reason why. We made the outward journey via Lyons, Brindisi and Salonika, but an armistice with Bulgaria was signed on September 29th, with Turkey on October 30th, with Austria-Hungary on November 3rd— and before Christmas we were travelling home via Corinth, Brindisi and Lyons. Release from the Forces finally came in May, 1919.

Still not twenty years of age I returned home to my parents who were now in charge of the Salvation Army corps at Batley in Yorkshire. Here we had an immense hall, then the largest building in the town and known as the 'Batla Castle'. My first need was for work, but the more doubtful aspects of my military novitiate were no recommendation in civvy street. However, I found employment in Leeds and, from force of habit, took my place in the Batley Corps as a bandsman. I could hardly do otherwise. Like many another serviceman in both world wars, I had been shown much kindness by Salvationists. In any case, I had little experience of any other form of church life. I had grown up in the Army, and perhaps non-Salvationists can hardly realise the intense loyalty of the rank and file to the Army. (This may be one reason why those who do leave feel an overwhelming compulsion to justify themselves.) So in the providence of God, in the Army I remained, though there may have been small personal credit due to me for that.

About this time I began to read more widely although too readily following the devices and desires of my own heart. I embarked on my private explorations without knowing how to explore, nor even the name of the country I was seeking. For all the technical skills acquired, service life had not stretched me mentally. Orders were obeyed, saluting smartly on receiving the word of command, but one was never such a nut case as to go looking for work to do. At my final posting at Strathbeg before demobilisation, my sole duty had been to monitor the twelve noon time signal and to advise the station adjutant's office and the officers' mess accordingly. My working day was then over. Authority was not at fault. Authority had next to nothing for me to do and was trying to get rid of me—and all like me—as fast as possible. Yet even this unsought sinecure became a weariness to the flesh and the current prospect of occupying an office stool in perpetuity was not alluring.

One Sunday evening in the summer of 1919 I was sitting at the organ in the Batley hall ready to accompany one of the congregational songs. My father was leading the meeting when a short sentence formed itself in my mind: 'This is what you ought to be doing.' Now I had no ambition to become any kind of public figure. I had never spoken in a meeting in my life save to utter the brief conventional testimony. Indeed, one of the humiliating experiences of my teenage years occurred when a divisional commander, out of the kindness of his heart, invited me to accompany him to a small corps in the neighbourhood. In the Sunday evening meeting I was asked to speak and obediently stood to my feet, but after a lapse of seconds sat down again without uttering a word.

Unwilling to draw attention to myself, I told no man of what has been described as 'God's disturbing call'. Without the knowledge of my parents, though it would have given them the greatest pleasure, I applied to be considered as a candidate for officership. When they heard from another source of what

I had done and gently chided me, I could only blame my absurd diffidence. The railway strike in the late autumn prevented my sharing in the opening of the first full length post-war session, but on Tuesday, October 7th, I boarded one of the first Leeds/King's Cross trains to run and presented myself to the Men's Wing of the International Training Garrison in Linscott Road, Clapton, E.5.

This had been the London Orphan Asylum, purchased by William Booth in 1882, and thereafter adapted and extended. The one hundred men cadets of this particular session were housed in three Victorian dwellings on a site in the Lower Clapton Road now occupied by the London Electricity Board. We slept in open dormitories and marched to and from Linscott Road before breakfast and after supper each morning and evening respectively. A half-day on Monday was the one weekly break. Every Sunday, and on Wednesday and Saturday afternoons as well, we marched to and from what were known as our training corps where we engaged in such activities as visitation, *War Cry* selling, open-air meetings, children's meetings and adult meetings. Up to Christmas my group of cadets marched to and from Poplar; after Christmas to and from Walthamstow. In the classroom we gave ourselves to the study of the Bible, Christian doctrine, Salvation Army principles and procedure, the leadership of public gatherings and the preparation of addresses. We also shared in the well-attended Thursday night holiness meetings in the Congress Hall. At this time the Army in London was still Clapton centred, and *The War Cry* reported that on Thursday, November 20th, 1919, the first public appearance of Commissioner T. Henry Howard (the retired Chief of the Staff) after his world tour drew a congregation of nearly four thousand.

Though as cadets our goings out and our comings in were strictly supervised, there was much to learn on both sides of the Clapton walls.

Without was the phenomenon of 'the followers'—a totally new experience for me. In the drab urban jungle of the London boroughs one of the easiest, and cheapest, of kicks was to be

obtained by creating a minor scene in an Army ⌐⌐⌐⌐⌐⌐⌐
preferably when cadets were present. This could be ⌐⌐⌐⌐⌐⌐
noisy invasion of the hall after a gathering had comm⌐⌐⌐⌐
or by chatting loudly to one's neighbour during any qu⌐⌐ ⌐⌐
moments, or by rising to one's feet to signal to a fancied
acquaintance on the other side of the building, or by simulating
a faint, or by slowly and deliberately processing to the door at
the beginning, middle, or end of the Bible address, or even by
coming forward to the Mercy Seat as the benediction was
about to be pronounced. As the session progressed these small
groups—mostly teenage girls, though some were in their
twenties—came to be known by sight, a few even by name.
They were the sad product of a dead-end environment and
their own inner inadequacies. Their ill-disguised aim was to
draw the maximum attention to themselves, though few were
sufficiently attractive to hold any roving eye. What can be said
in their favour is that they came to the Army. Few would have
attempted—or even wanted—to enter any of the traditional
churches; perhaps few congregations would have tolerated
them.

Without was also the annual Self-Denial appeal, an effort
which I had known from my youth up, though not of the
variety in which we cadets were called upon to engage. The
bane of the women cadets was the City and 'West End'
collecting; for the men of that session it was 'bus jumping'.
Two of us were given a map of the London General Omnibus
Company and bidden prepare a plan of action by which every
route would be tapped at some point within the metropolitan
area. With modest pride I completed my assigned task and
presented my draft to the authorities. My reward was to be
chosen as one of the company who would board an allotted
route and collect from the passengers. There were still a few
'pirate' buses in the city who turned a blind eye to our activities,
but we were given short shrift by the regulars. The experiment
was called off after two days and I spent the rest of the Self-
Denial period pounding the unsalubrious pavements of Notting
Hill.

As for life within, the medical arrangements at Clapton

provided an intriguing variant to what we had known in the Forces. I am sure that, had any man been taken seriously ill, professional medical attention would have been instantly forthcoming. But for those ailments, real or imaginary, for which the sick parade remedy had been a 'no. 9' or 'M. & D.', the Clapton cure was 'the hydro'.

In this we were legatees of the Army Mother's (Mrs. William Booth's) faith in water treatment. The first ever edition of 'Orders and Regulations for Officers', dated 1886, carried an appendix over her name stating that 'some considerable experience and observation have satisfied us that there is no system of treatment so effectual in curing disease or preventing serious consequences', and complaints from constipation to cholera were listed as responding to its benefits. As recently as 1946 a shortened appendix, this time minus the by-line, declared that 'every officer should procure some handy guide to homeopathy and hydropathy', and advised that 'in most English speaking countries Colman's mustard bran could be obtained by ordering it at the stores or hydropathic establishments.'

More from curiosity than genuine necessity I professed my need of this treatment and deservedly fell into the hands of Shepherd Drake Pennick, veteran sergeant at the Congress Hall, former London policeman, and at this time duty officer at the hydro. The treatment had the merit of simplicity and was in some respects a primitive forerunner of the now fashionable sauna. After immersion up to the neck in a bath of (according to the textbook) not less than 104°, one was ordered out against the wall to benefit from a prolonged jet of ice-cold water from Sergeant Pennick. In theory I was prepared for this, but not for the accompanying theological parallel which the Sergeant drew between this outward cleansing of the body and the inner sanctification of the spirit. I knew when I was beaten. He had me on the hip. In that setting I could not dispute with him and left the hydro suitably chastened.

There were also valuable lessons to be learnt from my fellow cadets. We were drawn from right across the board and this was one of the merits of training. As our faces differed, so did our latent powers. Who would have prophesied that Harold Littler, at whose table I sat for meals, would sail for the Far East on commissioning and spend the rest of his active service (including internment during the Second World War) in the same area? Or that Will Harrison, twenty-five years later in charge of cadets' education at the training college (by this time at Denmark Hill), would be cut off in his prime? Or that H. J. S. Guntrip would so soon embark on a ministerial career and become an accepted authority on the borderlands which conjoin the Christian faith and mental health? Or that at the age of twenty-six, after four-and-a-half years' service, Charles Brister would die on the mission field in China? Or that William F. Curl would command thirty-five corps in the British Territory during his forty-two years of officership? Well might every training officer take to heart the saying that 'thou knowest not whether shall prosper, either this or that'.

I became aware of my own Laodicean outlook in a meeting of men cadets which I attended on the evening of my arrival when the example of a comrade named Pinder was held up for our emulation. During his free time on the previous afternoon he had journeyed to Mile End Waste and, fired by the example of William Booth, had addressed himself on the way home to a group of navvies engaged in road repairs. Their discourteous rejoinder was to turn a handy hosepipe on him, soaking him to the skin. I could but reflect that I did not yet share his spirit.

The lesson was underscored as familiar names in Salvation Army life became real persons. John Lawley, Elijah Cadman, John A. Carleton, William Ridsdel (senior of all in service), were still in the land of the living. We listened to Mildred Duff, to Frederick St. George de Lautour Booth-Tucker, to Samuel Brengle, each of whom esteemed the reproach of the Army greater riches than the treasures of the Victorian establishment. Our Training Principal, Commissioner Hugh Whatmore, had been a member of the first brass band to be formed at Whitechapel, the Army's no. 1 corps. Lieut.-Colonel A. G. Cunningham, who had been the Army's representative on the 'Life and Work' and 'Faith and Order' committees which preceded the founding of the World Council of Churches, was in charge of the Men's Side—and when he spoke it was a foolish cadet who dared bark. He was supported by Major Robert Peat, one of whose exegetical master strokes was inspired by the comment of the blessed apostle Paul that he had sought 'to have always a conscience void of offence toward God'. Declared the Major, 'Some of you men possess a conscience void of any fence at all!' His sally was greeted in the spirit with which it was uttered.

Towering above all was General Bramwell Booth. The older generation revered him, this side idolatry, more than any man save his father. As was inevitable, most of us who had come out of the Forces saw him only from afar and never spoke to him. Maybe none of us wished—as the future General Orsborn was once told—to come and 'have his bones scraped'. Now and again some portentous word would be dropped as to how much longer one pair of shoulders could sustain the burden of world leadership—but 1929 was hidden from our eyes. We lesser mortals but watched and wondered—wondered what was on those scraps of paper which he sometimes scribbled while actually addressing a meeting; wondered at the way he could cut down some waffling speaker to size—and, when necessary, sit him down as well; wondered at his choice of the portion for the day from *The Soldier's Guide* to serve as the basis for an impromptu devotional talk; and, when a meeting was dying of dullness, wondered at the skill with which he would bring it back to life with one of his own early day stories which would have his hearers in the aisles while he looked on, benignly pleased, ready to make his devastating point while our guard was still dropped.

When my commissioning as a Probationary Lieutenant came round on Monday, May 3rd, 1920, and I was appointed as second officer to Blackpool, I was not the young man in the flying machine who had entered Clapton eight months earlier. But my education as a Salvation Army officer was only beginning. No bright light ever shone on my Damascus road, but I was slowly unlearning the tawdry values acquired during the previous two years. It might not be inaccurate to describe this slow turn around as my 'conversion'—though not 'sudden in a minute' was all accomplished. The hardest part of my training was about to commence.

3

Make Proof of Thy Ministry

THE HARDEST PART of my training—and it is not completed even yet! I had now to learn not by listening or reading but by doing. As an athlete has to take to the track or a musician to the concert-hall platform to gain needful experience, so the cure of souls can be undertaken only in real life situations. No practitioner ever concludes this un-ending apprenticeship in which heart, head and hand are united. As a stool needs three legs to stand evenly, an officer needs three firm bases for his life's work. He must be a man of God, a man of the Word and a man of the people.

If the last is taken first, this is because only one thing can be dealt with at a time. I had a very, very great deal to learn in all three. To be able to confirm my people in their faith I had first to stand in their shoes. Here temperament was a handicap. Neither life in the forces nor life in the training college had turned me into an extravert. I was still reluctant to butt in on anyone else's affairs and could not bring myself to frame so blunt a question as: 'Are you saved?' Intimate enquiries of that nature seemed to call for a more oblique approach. I did not rejoice in these inhibitions; how to be delivered from them was my problem.

Upbringing was also a handicap—not on account of its nature but its pattern. I had been reared in an officer's home. Until my late teens my corps officers had been my parents. Our domestic habits were determined by the corps programme.

It was taken for granted that the requirements of Salvation Army service came first. I knew nothing of a life where the inexorable demands of daily employment might conflict with the call of corps duty. So I had to learn that my soldiers had their living to earn, the standard of their home to maintain, their children to educate and their domestic budget to balance. Salvation Army soldiership was but one of the many demands upon their time, their strength and their money.

Nevertheless the determining word was—and is—soldiers. There are names which appear on Salvation Army rolls as adherents, friends, or recruits—but the majority are soldiers, and those who bear this New Testament title know that a nominal membership is not enough. These Christian soldiers belong to a militant task force which, under the great Captain of their salvation, is dedicated to fighting the good fight of faith. The Christian discipline which they accept is their perceptive response to the example of their Lord. This is no behaviour pattern forced upon them against their better judgment. In any case there is no process, civil or ecclesiastical, which could so coerce them. This is a way of life, freely offered and then fully accepted, which seeks to translate the spirit of Jesus into contemporary terms. This I understand to be the essence of the experience of holiness—a relationship with God which expresses itself in a distinctive pattern of living. The salvation soldier seeks to live to the glory of God, which means that he will not allow himself in any occasional practice, let alone a settled habit, which might cause his brother to stumble. This is to set his sights high—too high for mortal flesh, some may say. But with Christ as Saviour and Lord he can do no less. Lest this attitude be dismissed as the narrow fanaticism of a minor group of religious eccentrics, let God be praised that there is always a saving remnant who take their faith seriously. For if it is not to be taken seriously, why bother with it at all ?

Not yet twenty-one, much of this was seen through a glass darkly—mercifully so, else I could have been overwhelmed before I had even begun. But my first twelve months as a second officer at Blackpool was a dream of delight. True, wind and wave permitting, we were required to hold three open-air

meetings five days a week during the summer season on the
sands. (At the weekend we had the support of the corps
sections.) That was enough to give any healthy young man a
healthy appetite three times a day. No wonder the corps officer
and his wife in whose quarters I lived charged me a whole
guinea weekly out of my princely allowance of twenty-seven
shillings and sixpence—less deductions for national health
insurance, officers' pension fund and corps cartridge. But
this was far from penury. I had known that in the Forces when,
on enlistment, my pay as an 'erk' was a shilling a day, out of
which I was allowed to make an allotment of sixpence a day
to my mother. This left me with three shillings and sixpence
a week for riotous living in the dry canteen. But at Blackpool
I was rich in a far more rewarding sense for the officers shared
with me not just their table, but their public ministry, which
meant that in any three consecutive Sundays I addressed
a morning and an evening congregation many of whom
were old enough to be my parents. They bore me no ill will—
not openly expressed at any rate. Quite a number even encouraged me. Their kindness is not forgotten. A pat on the
back is never more welcome than in youth.

Then came my first corps in charge—Millhill, a suburb
of Blackburn. Here I discovered what later I was to re-discover
from that master realist, John Bunyan, how mixed is the
regiment of Christ's soldiers. Not that mine was a regiment;
not even a company; a couple of platoons maybe—no more.
If among them there were a Mr. Standfast, a Christiana and
a Mercy, there were also a Mr. Ready to Halt, Mr. Feeble-
mind and Much Afraid, Despondency's hapless daughter.
But if the one thought so little of his mind as to suggest it
be buried under a dunghill, and if nobody could ever understand what the other was singing, each in his way was determined to see the end of a Christian's journey. Happily,
the Salvationist has never forgotten the apostolic word to
'comfort the feebleminded'. At one time *The War Cry*
made 'Silly Billy' a weekly cartoon figure from whose lips
came words of wisdom. It may not have been realised that
we were actually keeping Wordsworth company.

She looks again—her arms are up—
She screams—she cannot move for joy;
She darts, as with a torrent's force,
She almost has o'erturned her horse,
And fast she holds her idiot boy . . .

She kisses o'er and o'er again
Him whom she loves, her idiot boy;
She's happy here, is happy there . . .
Her limbs are all alive with joy.

In the love of Betty Foy for her mentally retarded Johnny is to be seen the love of God for His spiritually retarded children.

At Millhill then, I led the eight-piece band; played the principal cornet—not of skill but of necessity; conducted three indoor meetings each Sunday—save for the help of the occasional special; acted as corps sergeant-major; attended to the corps accounts and made up the corps cash book with the help of Mercy, the corps secretary, who because of her years could provide me daily with the elements of a midday meal without causing public scandal. It was not her fault that after five months of such living I succumbed to jaundice. Even while laid on one side unexpected word arrived that I was to be taken from corps work and made responsible for divisional accounts—which I did in two divisions, the North-west and the Northern, when I married and with my wife was appointed to Chatham.

Even before the First World War the name of Bandmaster James Lee, of Warrington, was well-known in Salvation Army circles, and his family inherited his loyalty to the Movement. His daughter, Bessie, gained a first-class honours degree at the University of Manchester in 1915, and was an early representative of that ever increasing company who find that academic skills prove no hindrance to service beneath 'the yellow, the red and the blue'. In due course she resigned her appointment in what was then the John Howard Secondary

School, Clapton, and entered the training garrison two streets away. We were married in the Newcastle City Temple on November 17th, 1925. Our weekly salary for the first years of our life together was £2 9s. 6d.—but we had our riches.

Our one and only material treasure was a Bechstein upright which my wife had brought with her. She sang; I played only moderately—but our joint pleasure was always a means of refreshment. Nor could our limited means rob us of our love of beauty, whether in the world around us—which was for free, or in the chosen treasures on our bookshelf, to purchase which we had needed to count the cost. Between the winter of 1926 and the spring of 1941 we had four children. Parents will know their almost painful anxiety that every member of the family shall be sound in mind and limb. A handicapped child must be a test of religious faith and human affection. There are parents who triumph in this agonising adversity. All honour to them. Mercifully, we were not so tested, and in due course each of the four graduated—two in London, one at Oxford and one in Sydney (Australia).

Like my parents, we moved from corps to corps—though only for the first ten years of our married life. This is a demanding life-style for any woman who is a home lover, for she does not choose the town where she is to live nor the house she will occupy. Usually a wife and mother will build up her home over the years piece by piece but, save for her personal possessions which she may carry around, the officer-wife has no choice in what she finds. Her new quarters (as the official home of an officer is officially known) may be above reproach, but it is a fact of life that as no two men have exactly the same taste in ties, no two women favour exactly the same colour scheme. This is no one's fault. It would be appalling if every quarters was the same in every detail as its neighbour. At the same time, there can be situations which call for at least the temporary appreciation of that which may not immediately commend itself to the eye.

Despite these minor hazards it was good for us to range together from the Channel Islands to the Clydeside in this unique form of service in which husband and wife work as one. Brigadier A. may be appointed divisional commander for the Cumbrian division, and Commissioner B. to be territorial commander for Westralia, but Captain *and* Mrs. C. will be sent to take charge of the corps at Middletown. This turns out to be not only for the good of the work but for the good of their marriage as well, insofar that they share not merely their leisure—which is all many husbands and wives can do—but their vocation also. Both have accepted the same calling. Both are trained for that calling. All that Captain does Mrs. Captain can do as well. She does not sit in the congregation but shares with her husband the Salvation Army equivalent of the pulpit—the platform. Captain will rejoice that Mrs. Captain is no cipher. Mrs. Captain will rejoice that she is no dumb piece of platform decoration. Any who scoff at this as starry eyed should open their copy of *Far From the Madding Crowd* and read again what Thomas Hardy wrote about the final relationship between Bathsheba Everdene and Gabriel Oak.

This good fellowship . . . usually occurring through similarity of pursuits, is unfortunately seldom added to love between the sexes because men and women associate, not in their labours, but in their pleasures merely. Where, however, happy circumstance permits its development, the compounded feeling proves itself to be the only love which is as strong as death—that love which many waters cannot quench, nor the floods drown, beside which the passion usually called by that name is evanescent as steam.

My training in my calling continued. Some lessons were palatable; some were not; all were needful. I had to learn to keep my cool so that, whatever disagreements arose, I would never be on such bad terms with any of my people that I could not visit them in their homes or kneel with them in prayer. I repeat: this I had to learn—the hard way, for nothing does more damage to an officer's ministry than a breach which determines which homes he visits and which he does not.

I had to learn not to expect my say-so to carry the immediate judgment of all and sundry, and consequently not to abandon hastily any scheme which did not win an instant one hundred per cent support.

I had to learn to bear with those of the faithful who felt slighted if their own well-tried ways were seemingly by-passed by some new venture.

I had to learn that a plan which succeeded at A would not of necessity succeed at B. No two corps are alike. Internal resources are rarely the same. Age groupings vary from place to place. Soils change with the situation—which means that an address which here bore fruit thirtyfold or even sixtyfold might fall on stony ground there. So I had to learn to be willing to learn.

I had to learn to keep a confidence—whether given by one of my leaders or one of my soldiers. Only in this way could I mingle freely with my comrades and not fear the chance remark of any.

I had also to learn not to denigrate those to whom I was responsible in the presence of those for whom I was responsible. I learnt in due course that this rule applies at all levels, and he who breaks it is almost invariably repaid in his own coin. The measure a man metes is measured to him again.

I had to learn as well that if I had not asked to be appointed to X, neither had the corps at X asked for my appointment. If each new corps is virtually an unknown quantity to the new officer, so is he to the corps. The new arrival may expect to hear at least once during the early period of his command: 'You can't do that there 'ere!' And he will be a more than prudent man if, in some unguarded moment, part of an opening policy statement to the corps council does not run: 'Now in my last appointment this proved to be one of the most successful schemes the corps had undertaken for the previous five (ten, twenty or thirty, according to imagination) years.'

Most of all did I learn to honour the local officers and soldiers for their faithfulness. They stood by their corps for better, for worse. Nor were they ashamed of a faith which singled them out from other men. It is not unfair to say that were John Boyd a churchman his religious affiliation would excite little attention. But because he is a Salvationist a press photograph will show him in uniform complete with tuba. Of such stuff are our soldiers made. This is as well, for I learnt that if corps life prospers, the work of God as a whole prospers. An obvious illustration of this is that most candidates for officership are drawn from the corps level. This is not to ignore those who come directly from our social services but even they will have been influenced by officers who, in the first instance, came from corps life. But we shall not raise candidates even to staff our social services—praised though these be by the general public—unless the soil of our corps is warm enough and rich enough to nourish the delicate seed of an initial personal dedication.

The importance of a healthy corps life applies to the work of Christian evangelism as well. High level inter-denominational discussions of this subject at some selected international centre are doubtless of value. But those in attendance are for the most part already convinced of the need to proclaim Christ and Him crucified as the Saviour of the world, else they would not be there. But do not the conference statements and press releases on the primacy of evangelism sadly grow fainter and fainter as they reach the ears of the local congregation or the local corps? We Salvationists must not succumb to the illusion that a principle becomes an actuality simply by being headlined in the world's press, or broadcast over the world's networks, or—with the greatest respect—repeated worldwide by a General. I speak from experience.

Salvationists have a strong loyalty to their own corps. We believe in working on site. There is both a worthy and a less worthy side to this. Two corps in the same town can regrettably be bad neighbours. At the same time, they are more likely to work together if they can be persuaded to plan together. Would it not therefore be more fruitful if those in Perth (Western Australia), or in Kingston upon Hull (Humberside), or in Vancouver (British Columbia) could foregather in Perth, Hull and Vancouver to plan for concerted evangelism in Perth, Hull and Vancouver respectively? Two essential pre-requisites would be known to each group—the ground to be covered and the extent of their pooled resources. And at the end of the day they would be able to see for themselves how effectively—or otherwise—their works had been joined to their faith. No world figure would need to be flown in to point that out. Those first-hand conclusions would be weightier than any pronouncement from a distant Sinai.

T. W. Manson's words still remain true.

The Christianity that conquered the Roman Empire was not an affair of brilliant preachers addressing packed congregations. We have, so far as I know, nothing much in the way of brilliant preachers in the first three hundred years of the Church's life. There were one or two brilliant controversialists, but I suspect they made more enemies than friends; and the greatest of them all, Origen, was probably over the heads of most people most of the time . . . When we try to picture how it was done we seem to see domestic servants teaching Christ in and through their domestic service, workers doing it through their work, small shopkeepers through their trade, and so on, rather than eloquent propagandists swaying mass meetings of interested enquirers.

It is still true that the best propaganda for genuine Christianity is genuine Christians; and the New Testament is full of declarations of the convincing power, not of the spoken word, but of the lived life. Indeed, I think it is fair to say that the lives of Christians will have to be the parables of the Kingdom for the twentieth century.

So there is nothing new about the people speaking to the people. What has changed is the character of the parties involved. In the world of the New Testament most men were religious, each after his own fashion. Today it is a truism to say that there is a widespread rejection of the need for any form of faith. This is largely a passive rejection—but none the less effective for that. Genuine individual conversions still occur—and may their number increase—but the most successful of mass rallies or the best-attended suburban ministry cannot hide the fact that the decently godless are in the majority. So while, for example, public support for the work of The Salvation Army may increase annually, what proportion of the givers personally accept the gospel which the Army exists to proclaim? John Doe may give a coin from his purse to the Lord's work but how often his heart to the Lord?

What has also changed within the Army is the salvation soldier himself. In my boyhood there still lived those who could answer the taunt concerning the credibility of our Lord's action in changing water into wine with the reply: 'Well, He changed all my beer into furniture.' The story was still in circulation of the currently prosperous Salvationist who kept in a bedroom cupboard the ragged clothes (duly cleaned, of course) which he was wearing when he first knelt at the Mercy Seat, so that any temptation to foolish pride might instantly be put to flight by this visible reminder of the horrible pit and the miry clay from which he had been rescued. Most of today's bandsmen and songsters have no such dramatic testimony to give. Nevertheless they have a genuine testimony— one centring around God's prevenient grace which is also part of his divine work for us men and for our salvation. No lad is required to waste his substance in riotous living in order fully to know Jesus as Saviour. So we may return thanks that many of our young people have never wandered into the far country. Even as I work over the first draft of this chapter *The Musician* announces that a third generation Salvationist has been engaged as the principal trombone in the Hallé Orchestra, and that another is about to read for the Honours School of Jurisprudence at Oxford—though there is nothing new in a Salvationist at Oxbridge at this time of day.

It therefore follows if, as an officer, I am to be a man of my people, much more is demanded of me now than half a century ago. To the Salvation Army officer's traditional capacity to meet material or spiritual need has to be added the capacity to meet current intellectual needs. This increased responsibility, at the time no more than a cloud like a man's hand, was discerned by General Albert Orsborn in an article which he

wrote for the July, 1928, issue of *The Staff Review*.* The then
Chief Side Officer for men at the International Training
Garrison quoted with approval some sentences written by the
editor himself in the previous issue that:

> the average corps officer is not sufficiently in advance (if
> abreast) of the general average of our better educated
> soldiery as regards intelligence, knowledge and experience,
> to command their respect and confidence as a leader,
> teacher and guide, however warmly they may regard him
> for his goodness and devotion.

The singling out of 'the corps officer' as a class apart is to
be regretted; we are all under a measure of condemnation. To
be a man of the people in a technological age means that I
myself must at least be as skilled in the cure of souls as are the
members of my flock in their several occupations and pro-
fessions. It is not just hungry sheep who look up and are not
fed. We have wrongly supposed that the adjective silly always
goes with the noun sheep. Those who look up—as and when
they do—are hungry fitters, hungry draughtsmen, hungry
shop assistants, hungry mothers of families, hungry teachers,
hungry bright young things, unskilled yet hungry labourers,
hungry shop stewards, hungry dockhands, hungry office
workers, hungry railwaymen and hungry graduates. I am not
required to be a master of their various occupations or pro-
fessions but, before God, I am required to know my own work
as well as they know theirs. Much is required nowadays of
him who desires to be a man of the people in order that he may
minister in Christ's name to the people. He may not be called
to walk with kings of whom but few are left, but he is called
to walk the new housing estate, the market square, the shop
floor, the city centre for a due part of six days in the week in
order that he may be equipped to stand on his platform on the
seventh. Like his Lord, he must be touched with the feeling
of his people's infirmities. The street as well as his study has
a part to play in enabling him to speak to their condition.

*A private magazine circulating among staff officers, commenced by General
Bramwell Booth in 1922 but discontinued at the end of 1931.

4

The Good Word of God

BUT HE HAS also to be a man of the Word, and this second demand is harder still to meet.

In a superficial way I had known the leading Bible stories from my youth up. No one could have regularly attended the Army's young people's meetings without having learnt about Abraham and Isaac, Jacob and Esau, Moses and Aaron, Samuel and Saul, David and Solomon, Elijah and Elisha, Daniel and Jonah, together with the principal events in the life of our Lord and the principal incidents in the travels of the apostle Paul. The discerning reader will perceive that the omissions in my list are as significant as the inclusions. But at that age one read, for the most part, without overmuch imagination and the brutalities of Old Testament warfare, as well as the dubious behaviour of some of the characters involved, left us untroubled. In any case, only the King James Version was then available, and its Elizabethan English could as readily veil as reveal the depravity of human nature and the depth of human emotions. Moffatt had not yet written of Agag's 'tottering (N.E.B. 'faltering') steps', nor his cry: 'Death is a bitter thing'.

But this did not detract from the fascination of the Bible. As a boy of nine I contracted scarlet fever and one of the bedrooms in our quarters became my isolation ward. Since that day scarlet fever has lost many of its terrors, but a sheet steeped in carbolic hung over the bedroom door. No one came in or out save my mother, and she had to make liberal use of a solution of carbolic on entering and leaving. The entire room with its contents had to be fumigated on my recovery and no book or paper passed in was allowed out. This meant that my reading was limited to the Bible but I discovered for myself the story of Esther, the Jewish girl who concealed her race when she entered the royal harem of the Persian king but whose shrewdness and courage, when queen, saved her people from the vengefulness of that arch-antisemite, Haman. To a small boy this was a clear example of the well-deserved triumph of a goodie over a rascal of a baddie.

Later, like Molly Weir in *Best Foot Forward*, I fell under the spell of the language of the Bible. She has related how she would

> race along to school chanting: 'Tell it not in Gath, publish it not in the streets of Askelon, lest the daughters of the Philistines rejoice, lest the daughters of the uncircumcised triumph'. And as I turned the corner I wailed: 'Ye daughters of Israel, weep over Saul, who clothed you in scarlet and other delights, who put ornaments of gold upon your apparel.' What marvellous sounds they were!

My own reactions were more sober, for it was in a Sunday evening service at a kirk in Rothesay (where my father was convalescing after a long illness) that there fell on my ears like the grave tolling of a single bell: 'Or ever the silver cord be loosed, or the golden bowl be broken, or the pitcher be broken at the fountain, or the wheel be broken at the cistern.' Remembering my regular Sunday attendances, it is probable that I had heard those words more than once before, but this time I listened to them—and did not forget. Time slowly dissolved—and what lay beyond?

In my early teens I also became a corps cadet* and the record shows that on July 14th, 1916, I was awarded a first-class certificate with honours for the 'A' course of studies.

---

*A youth section designed to provide preliminary training for teenagers in Salvation Army service.

There is no evidence of further certificates, with or without honours. The seed, springing up quickly, could have withered as quickly. So with this limited equipment which my time in the Forces had done nothing to improve, I entered training where, to do the curriculum justice, we followed the advice of Lord Ickenham to Archie Gilpin when the latter confessed his difficulties in reducing his thoughts to ordered speech. 'Begin at the beginning', said his lordship encouragingly. 'Then work through from there to the middle and, taking your time, carry on to the end.' Sound advice! We began at the beginning, with Genesis 1:1 in fact, but our trouble was that we had not the time to take our time. The training session lasted approximately forty weeks. In reality it was a crash course for returned servicemen. The Bible-study plan provided for forty-five lessons on the Old Testament—with nine review periods, and forty lessons on the New Testament—with eight review periods.

(Before any wrong conclusions are drawn from these facts it should be remembered that these sentences refer to more than half a century ago and that teaching staff, methods and material have now improved out of all recognition.)

However, immediately after the First World War a certain imbalance could not be denied. The life of Moses and the liberation of Israel from Egypt up to their arrival at Kadesh Barnea occupied nine lessons, of which two were devoted to the Tabernacle (with due note of the coverings of goats' hair, rams' skins dyed red and badgers' skins) but Jonah, Amos, Hosea and Micah were encompassed in a single lesson. Isaiah was also given one lesson. Jeremiah was treated along with Jehoiakim, Jehoiachin and Zedekiah in another solitary lesson.

Treatment of the New Testament was similarly compressed, though fifteen lessons were devoted to the life and teaching of Jesus. The Epistles were dealt with more summarily. One lesson sufficed for what the index called Thessalonians and Corinthians; one for Galatians and Romans; one for Philemon, first and second Timothy and Titus; with one each for Hebrews, the General Epistles and the Revelation respectively.

Once again no one was to blame for this abbreviated study

plan. The staff did their utmost to cope with the varied
intellectual standards of the cadets and the shortness of time.
With similar desire to make the best of a difficult situation
they introduced us to the study of homiletics under the simpler
title of 'Subject Notes'. A thirty-two page booklet gave
examples of how to treat a selected scripture text or passage
by the method of enumeration, of extension, of expansion, by
synthesis or by analysis. Sample outlines were regularly submitted to our teachers though some of the men home from the
wars—with whom the pen was not at all times their mightiest
weapon—did not always treat these exercises with due
seriousness. It was rumoured that a former non-commissioned
officer submitted one of the Founder's outlines which had
earlier appeared in print. 'Not one of your best efforts', was
the teacher's written comment. Come to think of it, that was
a very perceptive judgment.

As the session wore on alarm and despondency seized me.
Suppose I was appointed to some tiny corps on my own. My
scanty barrel of meal and cruse of oil would soon be exhausted.
Mixing my metaphors, I hastily set to work to lay by some
shots in my locker. Shots? They might better be described
as damp squibs. Mercifully none was ever used, for I was
beginning to perceive the difference between a theoretical
exercise and that preparation of the mind and spirit which
was a genuine response to felt human need. So communing
with no heart save my own I made up my mind to try to
prepare some mini-talks to be used when called upon to speak
in cadets' open airs. Such opportunities were plentiful enough,
for we had three on a Sunday and one each Wednesday and
Saturday at our training corps, plus one on a Thursday evening
in any of the streets between Lower Clapton Road and Pembury
Road before the weekly holiness meeting in the Clapton
Congress Hall. In winter there were few listeners, but what
of it? At the moment all I was looking for was practice. And
if the street was feebly lit, so much the better. I wanted to
learn how to be independent of my barely decipherable notes
written on a post card and concealed in my song book. One
of our instructors had recently delivered himself of the

aphorism that a successful speaker would not have his head in
his notes but his notes in his head. If this was one way to end
waffling I would have a go!

It was some time before I came across A. N. Whitehead on
the need 'to render clear to popular understanding the eternal
greatness incarnate in the passage of temporal fact', but it was
to this still unclear goal that I was hesitantly addressing myself.
Happily I was working more wisely than I knew. I had no
idea that the future would present me with several years of
seaside appointments at Blackpool, Bournemouth and Jersey,
where I would be required to speak sometimes to a handful,
sometimes—God help me!—to a crowd of people, many of
whom rarely attended a place of worship at all. In *Crowded
Canvas* Canon Max Warren has written that he knows of no
better preparation for a preacher than for him to learn to
throw his voice across a beach while there is a high cross-wind
blowing and the surf breaking on the pebbles behind him.
Minus the surf on the pebbles I shared such an apprenticeship.

But help was at hand from three very different sources.
My first commanding officer was a devotee of Alexander
Maclaren, formerly of Union Chapel, Manchester, and
possessed a complete set of his *Expositions of Holy Scripture*—
mostly cast in sermonic form. Maclaren used few illustrations,
told no pithy anecdotes and made no concessions to the frailty
of the flesh. He even regarded the introduction of a soloist into
the Sunday evening service with dismay but, as George
Jackson once observed in his *Parson's Log* in *The Methodist
Recorder*, he could strike almost any text with the silver hammer
of his thought and, like Caesar's Gaul, it would fall into three
parts. I duly noted that the richer the thought the greater the
need for orderly expression.

At the moment mine was of the skim milk variety but, in
the providence of God, a second aid reached me. G. F.
Barbour's life of Alexander Whyte was published in 1923 and,
as he had died only two years earlier, his name and work were
still a power. I have forgotten the price of this biography but,
whatever it was, I have been repaid many times over. The

676 pages stand on my shelf of lives today. Dr. Whyte used to
say that his heart 'warmed to the red jersey of The Salvation
Army'. The heart of this lad of limited education, eager to
learn yet often bewildered how best to set about it, warmed
to this scholar-preacher and his interleaved Bible. Simple as
this may seem to the more academically qualified, to me it was
a revelation from on high. This was not a Bible into which
one's completed notes could be inserted in the appropriate
place for use at the appropriate time. This was a working Bible
for use in that place of hard labour—the study, though no
corps quarters I ever occupied possessed such a room set apart
for such a purpose. No matter; this was a Bible into which
every scrap of information about a word, a sentence, or a
passage could be entered against that word, sentence, or
passage. Almost with awe I gazed with the help of a magnifying
glass at a reproduction in the biography of opposing pages from
Whyte's own Bible. Among the jumble of handwritten notes
I could discern references—among others—to Browning's
Ring in the Book, Blougram's Apology, Samuel Rutherford,
the Abbé Grou, *The Atlantic Monthly*, Blaise Pascal, William
Law, Godet and A. B. Bruce.

Here then was confirmation of two clues—order and plenty.
I could teach myself to practise order. For plenty I would
need to work, for I knew enough to know that such spiritual
and intellectual manna would not fall unsought every morning.
So some friends gave me an inter-leaved Bible, since when
I made several of my own—the most fruitful of which were
inter-leaved gospels which were made by pasting incident by
incident, or saying by saying, from the four gospels to the top
right and left-hand corners of foolscap sheets, leaving plenty
of space for the information I hoped to acquire. Yet even
though I had dug the trench and laid the wood in my own
rough and ready fashion, how was any kind of acceptable
offering to be prepared for the altar?

While still a boy my mother had bidden me read a chapter
of the Bible every day—advice which I confess I found hard
to follow. Tracts of the Old Testament remained a desert drear.
Her large Bible, bearing her maiden name, Mary Jones, I still

possess. Published by the Oxford University Press with
'Notes analytical, critical, chronological, historical and geo-
graphical . . .', the two cross-reference columns on the page
headed 'The first book of Moses called Genesis' each carried
the note: 'Before Christ, 4004'. By chapter six the figure was
2448; by the opening of Exodus 1689; by the beginning of
Joshua 1451. I had not so much as heard of Archbishop Usher,
but, lest it be thought that my home was particularly obscuran-
tist, I recall that a twelve-volume encyclopedia hawked
around this country in the thirties carrying an introduction
by Dr. Cyril Norwood, then Headmaster of Harrow, and
prepared 'with the specialist assistance of over a hundred
experts', declared Usher's work to be 'the basis of the received
biblical chronology.' I had to resolve the nature of the hymn
of creation without their aid.

On leaving training I religiously set aside an early part of
each morning for the consecutive reading of Scripture, but
still the text refused to come alive. I had not yet found the clue
which would transform the Old Testament from a list of the
kings of Israel and Judah into what the Army's *Handbook of
Doctrine* calls 'a progressive revelation of God . . . culminating
in Jesus Christ.' And I also still needed a vantage point from
which the gospel story could be seen, not as a disconnected
description of certain parables and miracles, but as a related
whole.

For this I had to wait, for the demands of my several corps
appointments were continuous and exacting. It would be an
exaggeration to say that I had never a minute to call my own,
but there were never fewer than two public meetings on a
Sunday—most often three, and never fewer than two public
weeknight meetings. At St. Helier (C.I.) where my wife and I,
with our two young children, were stationed from May, 1930
to May, 1932, a normal Sunday began with knee-drill (the
Army word for prayer meeting) at 7.15 a.m., followed by an
open-air meeting at 10 a.m., the holiness meeting at 11 a.m.,
in the summer a beach meeting at 3 p.m., another open-air
at 6 p.m., the salvation meeting at 6.45 p.m. and, again in the
summer, a final open-air at the pier about 8.15 p.m. My wife

and I shared the principal indoor meetings on a Sunday, but the summer open-air meetings attracted such congregations as to demand at least an equal degree of preparedness. No preacher of the gospel could dare treat such opportunities lightly. Some readers may regard such a day as beyond the reasonable strength of any one man. But I was still in my early thirties, and if that testifies to comparative inexperience it also speaks of comparative youth.

My last corps, on the Clydeside, had three open-air and three indoor meetings on a Sunday, together with three weeknight meetings and two weeknight open-airs. The senior band was present at all the open-air meetings and all but one of the indoor gatherings, and the songster brigade at all the indoor meetings but one. Thus the commanding officer regularly faced the daunting prospect of saying something worthwhile six times each week. On reflection, it is not surprising that exhortation sometimes took the place of instruction. In addition these were depression years. One-third of the insurable population of the burgh were unemployed. When at last work was resumed on the *Queen Mary*, pipers played the first shift down to John Brown's gates. Families lacked not luxuries but necessities. Hunger marches were too frequent a spectacle. On occasion we slept them in our hall. They left it as they found it—not a seat out of place. Arising out of this, John McGovern, Labour M.P. for Shettleston, wrote:

I have during the whole of my life admired the members of The Salvation Army, and the splendid spirit of real Christianity which they display towards persons of every denomination as well as those who have no religious beliefs.

During the recent hunger marches to Edinburgh and London, I have had reason publicly to thank your officers and rank and file members for providing shelter for hundreds of unemployed men when accommodation had been refused from all other sources. The officers—men and women— remained up during the night attending to the hungry without a murmur but with a kind word for everyone.

In May, 1935, my wife and I farewelled from Clydebank and instead of taking my place behind the corps flag at the head of the march I now brought up the rear. I had become a backroom boy at International Headquarters charged with the duty of preparing the Bible lessons to be used in Salvation Army youth work at home and overseas. Now I was to discover from personal experience the difference between one's own choice of a scripture verse or passage as the basis for an address—which could be (hopefully) improved or discarded— and a mastery of the Bible as a whole. Since leaving training I had continued to read and study eagerly—but erratically. Like the Ethiopian on his way home from Jerusalem, I needed some man to guide me. At the training college almost every moment was supervised but, save for twelve months' compulsory study after commissioning, beginners were left very much to their own devices. (Again I must add that this situation has radically changed for the better in recent years.) At that time, however, though I might occasionally be asked what I was reading, rarely was any book outside the Army's own literature recommended to me. The book reviews which now occupy five or six pages of *The Officer* are of more recent introduction. So I had mostly to make my own way around and it is not surprising that every now and again I found myself in some dead end.

Then came a third source of help—consisting in the first place of the discovery of a comprehensive outline of the life of Christ, the work of Basil Redlich, which for the first time enabled me to see our Lord's life steadily and to see it whole. I should have been able to work this out for myself from a harmony of the gospels—yet did not. But the single-spaced pages I typed out from Redlich are still with me.

In the second place I read an announcement that Dr. C. Ryder Smith was to give a series of evening lectures on the Old Testament at the University of London. The fee was nominal. The long-range gain was immense, for a door was flung open not only upon the biblical knowledge of the lecturer himself but upon the work of many other scholars in the same field. The harvest was truly plenteous and I am still reaping. Who begat who was seen to be of small account set beside the insights of the prophets who linked religion with life and declared that the worship of God was indissolubly linked with justice between men.

Once again this may sound elementary to those who have enjoyed a formal theological education, but it was the kiss of life to me. In my earlier indiscriminate reading I had known a few biblical scholars by name. I had heard some praised as fundamentalist and others damned as modernist. I did not wish to wear either of those question-begging labels. The only 'ist' by which I wanted to be known was Salvationist. All the more reason why I welcomed this new light upon the Word. My faith was not weakened but confirmed. My personal experience of Jesus as Saviour and Lord was not endangered but deepened. I felt a heightened sense of privilege that I could lay this clearer understanding of the ways of God with men upon the altar and wait for the fire to fall upon the offering. My desire to see men truly converted unto God did not wane but burned more steadily. The deeply evangelical passages in the Old Testament came alive as never before.

Many a time in a salvation meeting I had used Fanny Crosby's lines:

> Though your sins be as scarlet
> They shall be as white as snow—

but now it became plain that the sins for which pardon was freely offered were not simply individual transgressions, though these were included. A whole way of life was being indicted. What was rotten in the state of Judah was the gulf between rich and poor; the practice of bribery; the consequent corruption of justice; the indifference of the leaders of the day to this state of affairs and, worst of all, the presence of the men guilty of these sins of commission and omission in the Temple worship, blandly assuming that they could deceive God as easily as they had deceived their fellows.

There was no holding me. Page after page of what had been a wilderness of words in the Old Testament blossomed abundantly. I began to grasp what the prophets were saying to their contemporaries and what, by the Spirit, they were saying to us. I rejoiced to discover that the Army Mother had quoted Isaiah (1:4) in this vein in one of her St. James' Hall addresses* and, in a later series of similar meetings, had spelled out the truth more plainly still.

Stories come to me from Hackney Wick, Seven Dials, St. Giles', the Borough and other parts ... of men and women nearly naked, children absolutely so, women who must not look up from their matchbox making at 2½d. per gross, or their shirt stitching at 3d. each, for fear of reducing their earnings by a half-penny, thus robbing their children of an ounce more bread ... Thousands of such wretched beings are living ... perhaps not two hundred yards from this very spot where we are assembled this afternoon, and yet who cares for them ? ... You London Christians, what shall you say in the great day of account ?†

Again, I saw how Amos rose above the popular but mistaken conception of his day of a God who cared for Israel but for none else, and whose sole business was supposedly to vindicate the chosen race against all comers. But this inspired country-man declared that the people of Ethiopia were as dear to God as the people of Israel and, if He had been behind their deliverance from Egypt, had He not also inspired the migration of the Philistines from Crete and the Syrians from Mesopotamia ? In twentieth-century terms, is not the immigrant population in Britain (with all their faults) as dear to Him as the indigenous population (with all their faults) ?

And with what delight did I find Samuel Brengle saying in his last published article in *The Officers' Review*:

Read the Old Testament gospel of Jonah. As you read, forget the whale and see God ... God has the first and last

*Papers on Godliness, pp. 50 and 51.
†Popular Christianity, pp. 155 and 156.

word in the book, and he who reads and laughs is a fool unless he laughs for very joy.

I was now reading 'for very joy' and have so sought to continue believing, as did John Robinson, pastor to the Pilgrim Fathers, that 'the Lord has more truth yet to break forth out of His holy word'.

5

Perfecting Holiness in the Fear of God

THE THIRD ESSENTIAL—to be 'a man of God'—is as hard to attain as it is difficult to define. 'Not as though I had already attained . . .' Not everyone is at home in the company of a man of God so it is much easier for stage and screen to turn him into a figure of fun—'all gas and gaiters'. Good for a laugh on the box. With some men their laughter turns to derision. They cannot hide their dislike of such a figure. He is a parasite on society. A cumberer of the ground. A third-class bread ticket is all he deserves. 'Awa' and work' is a cry that has greeted my ears from time to time. Yet there are others who feel in their bones that such a man—beside whom they prefer not to sit if another place is available in the crowded bus or train—is seeking to follow a way of life which reveals the limitations of their own. This ambivalence in public opinion is evidenced by the malicious delight which surfaces when some unhappy man of God yields to the love of money or the pleasures of the flesh. Because (in Browning's phrase) 'priests are only men', they can rise so gloriously or fall so disastrously.

This, in my sheltered ignorance, I had to learn—as I had to learn that the collapse of a man of God can have more than one cause. The seeming failure of his ministry can break his spirit. There is no measurable standard of cost-effectiveness which can be applied to his work. The best of seed will bring forth but little fruit on stony soil or thorny ground. Wrote a rural priest to Leslie Paul: 'A man can easily lose heart when Sunday after Sunday he is ministering to less than six people at any one service.'

The daily wear and tear of his charge can reduce a man to questioning his vocation. Recently I read in *The Officer* (a monthly magazine circulating among all English speaking officers throughout the world):

> How often is it recognised that the settling of corps disputes is the main drain on an officer's spiritual resources? It is not the man in the street who exhausts an officer. In an age that questions the role of religion we find a sense of satisfaction and even re-assurance in serving Mr. Everyman, importunate and untimely as his calls sometimes are.
>
> Nor is it the platform ministry which saps our spiritual resources . . . I recall General Wilfred Kitching remarking in officers' councils that God can renew the officer through the officer's own meeting preparation and delivery . . . But it is the bickering, the feuding, the falling out about nothing of importance, that can make us bitter and cynical. More, it can make us display that hasty temper which no amount of fine speaking can explain or gloss over.

Equally harassing can be a man's frugal domestic budget especially where, as in The Salvation Army, officers of a particular rank receive the allowances due to that rank—and nothing more. It is a tribute to the officer corps of the Army that the most gifted among them live by this egalitarian rule. No one makes anything on the side. This can press hardly on those with growing families, yet the basic integrity of the men and women through whose hands public money passes week by week is beyond reproach. There is virtually a fool-proof system of accounting and auditing in the Army, but this mostly serves to demonstrate that its practice could be suspended without loss—though this will not happen as honesty must not merely exist but be shown to exist.

At heart few men of God weary of serving their fellows.

But a man may begin to question whether he is doing this in the most fruitful way. So he casts around—considers the possibility of social service within the framework of local government, or whether he could not teach R. E. at school, or the likelihood of some administrative opening in one or other of the many charities now operating in this country. He is not in revolt against the Movement he is serving. In few instances is he possessed by any way-out theological ideas which he feels a messianic conviction to proclaim. As often as not it is just that the vision splendid has faded into the light of common day. The heroic for earth has proved too hard.

Most inexorable of all is the truth that the man of God can be tempted just like other men. No form of ecclesiastical preferment can guarantee him immunity. As human experience bears sorry witness, advancement can abet a man's downfall. He who thinks he stands has ever to take heed lest he fall. Hazards can beset a man—and a woman—even on the pathway of duty.

Brigadier Mary Scott has described the effect upon her own mind of a book of hard porn which she found among the belongings of a girl who came to her for food and shelter.* Snares can be deliberately laid for the feet of the godly. A husband and wife who had taken an unreasoning dislike to their spiritual pastor tried with malice aforethought to trap him in a compromising situation. More than one young man officer has found that Potiphar's wife is still around. Some years ago, in the course of a normal morning's visitation, I found myself listening to a married woman who, under the pretence of seeking counsel, launched into an explicit description of sexual intercourse with a casual visitor. The only possible action was to get to one's feet with all speed and, making for the door, to say: 'You will please excuse me, Mrs. X. I will come back later—with my wife.'

Men of God are flesh and blood. They would be small use to their fellows were they not. But they also 'belong to God' (N.E.B.), are 'God's servants' (Knox), are 'dedicated to God' (Jerusalem Bible). This dual relationship can produce its

*The Midnight Patrol by Phyllis Thompson (Hodder and Stoughton), ch. 12.

tensions but, thanks be to God, it is also the source of their salvation. So despite the most unexpected and violent squall, their anchor can hold.

Each of the historic churches has its own spiritual culture and terminology. It need cause no surprise that these aids vary. What matters is the end result. By their fruits are men known. As a lad I accepted without overmuch questioning the religious life style in which I was reared. Ours was a home where prayer was heard. Grace was said before all meals. Rarely an officer visitor left us for another appointment without prayer that he might be given 'travelling mercies'. The Arminian doctrine of John Wesley, as interpreted by William and Catherine Booth, was the sure word of truth. 'There is but one God,' William Booth used to say, 'and John Wesley is his prophet.' Wesley's phrase concerning 'the second blessing' became part of the Army's speech, and the Founder acknowledged his indebtedness in a letter to Bramwell dated August 27th, 1876, and which concluded:

I have been reading Tyerman's 'Wesley' during my illness and have, by comparing Wesley's experience with my own, derived some important lessons. One is that, under God, Wesley made Methodism not only by converting sinners but by making well-instructed saints. We must follow in his track or else we are a rope of sand . . . Let us profit by the experience of those who trod similar paths before us.

As with Wesley, William Booth realised that he was as much a learner as a teacher. This is clear from the letters which Catherine addressed to her mother. Husband and wife were still at 'Bethesda', Gateshead, when on February 4th, 1861, she wrote:

I have much to be thankful for in my dearest husband. The Lord has been dealing very graciously with him for some time past. His soul has been growing in grace, and its outward developments have been proportionate. He is now on full stretch for holiness. You would be amazed at the change in him.

Seven days later Catherine wrote that she had claimed the experience of sanctification by 'the simple reception of Christ as an all sufficient Saviour, dwelling in my heart and thus cleansing it from all sin . . . I have dared to reckon myself dead indeed unto sin, and alive unto God through Jesus Christ, my Lord.'

This was simplicity itself and, in Christian Mission doctrine, the corresponding article was equally simple. 'We believe that it is the privilege of all believers to be "wholly sanctified" and that "their whole spirit soul and body" may "be preserved blameless unto the coming of our Lord Jesus Christ".' Would that the well-meaning missioners of that day had been equally content. But some of them had to be tinkering. Article eight was changed from 'through grace by faith' to 'by grace through faith'. The 'endless punishment of the wicked' was altered to 'everlasting punishment' in 1875 and back to 'endless' in 1878.

Two years earlier Railton joined hands with William Garner—with whom he had earlier crossed swords—to dot the 'i's and cross the 't's of article ten. Railton has been described by one biographer as 'next to Catherine Booth, the first of the Army's theologians'. If 'first' here simply means in point of time, the comment can stand, but if it means first in competence, then the explanation which Garner and he added to article ten testifies against him.

We believe that after conversion there remain in the heart of the believer inclinations to evil or roots of bitterness, which, unless overpowered by divine grace, produce actual sin, but that these evil tendencies can be entirely taken away by the Spirit of God, and the whole heart thus cleansed from everything contrary to the will of God, or entirely sanctified, will then produce the fruits of the Spirit only. And we believe that persons thus entirely sanctified may by the power of God be kept unblamable and un-reprovable before Him.

Without doubt both men meant well but what they did was to lay hands upon a biblical figure of speech and forcibly transform it into a character judgment. The Old Testament source of this comparison is part of a speech attributed to Moses in which the Israelite leader made the point that the covenant with Him who had brought them out of the land of Egypt was binding upon all (Deut. 29:14–18). Anyone who sought to worship another god was 'a root from which springs gall and wormwood', that is to say, an influence for evil. The Epistle to the Hebrews used this phrase (12:14, 15) to warn members of the Early Church that any of their number who forfeited the grace of God was a 'bitter noxious weed growing up to poison the whole'. In other words, one bad apple could spoil the whole dish. This was a warning to a community and this is the explanation offered by the *New Testament Commentary* (Salvation Army edition, preface by William Booth). 'The writer has in view some individual instance of apostasy ... The defection of one member ... is a danger to the whole body.'

From 1881 to 1922, however, the paragraph quoted above was part of the text of the Army's articles of faith. In 1922 it was reduced to small print, and then relegated to a footnote in the 1935 edition of the *Handbook of Doctrine*. Finally, after a sitting of the Doctrine Council on November 16th, 1949, a recommendation was submitted to the General that this misleading analogy be omitted altogether, and this was done in the 1969 revision.

Meanwhile this figure of speech had been employed in some Salvation Army songs and certainly had formed the basis of many an address. On more than one Sunday morning these roots had been itemised and described—sometimes in detail. Even so sane a holiness teacher as the beloved Brengle would ask—as he did in 'The Way of Holiness'—'Are all the roots of bitterness gone?'

As a lad I grew up at a time when visiting officers to a corps

would 'test the meeting'. That is to say, before the customary
period of dedication and prayer brought the Sunday morning
gathering to a close, those present would be asked to witness—
either by standing to their feet or by raising a hand—that the
experience of holiness was theirs. The roots of bitterness had
been removed. This was always a moment of acute discomfort
for one teenager, tempered by the fact that, as his father had
bidden him accompany the congregational singing—by regulation the corps band played only for the opening song on
Sunday mornings—he had to remain seated at the organ.
His mistake was that he thought the desired witness meant
that he was so good that he could not be better. The word
'perfect' had him confused. Whatever else he was, he knew
he was not that. And in age he is still of the same opinion,
though now he understands that—in Wesley's phrase—'there
is no perfection . . . which doth not admit of perpetual increase. So that how much soever any man hath attained, or
in how high a degree a believer may be perfect, he hath still
need to grow in grace.' Nor has he forgotten reading a question
and answer which appeared in the minutes of Wesley's 1759
conference with his preachers in Bristol:

Q.   In what manner would you advise those who think they
have attained to speak of their own experience?
A.   With great wariness, and with the deepest humility
and self-abasement before God.

Over the years he has learnt that he was not the only per-
plexed adolescent. Hugh Redwood was also an adolescent
when he first met the Army in Bristol. In his autobiography,
Bristol Fashion, he wrote of his first reaction to the teaching
of holiness. 'I shrank from the word'—and continued:

Indeed, I shrink from it still because of the way in which
it is misused. Terms like holiness and sanctification . . .
should be charily used at all times, they come with singular
unfittingness from some of those who use them most freely;
men and women who, as I know to my sorrow, can be

bitter, vindictive and untruthful in dealings with those from whom they differ.

For my own part, I have never been—and still am not—given to dramatic resolutions but, as my work in the Literary Department at the Salvation Army's International Headquarters from 1935 onwards gave me increasing freedom to accept meeting invitations, I remembered my own silent bewilderment on Sunday mornings and purposed in my heart to speak of the experience of holiness as honestly and as intelligently as God should help me. As with most resolves of that sort, the results were mixed. In every company there are those who are at ease only with the familiar. To hear some well-remembered phrase is to be assured that the speaker is 'sound'. Old wine does not taste the same from a new bottle. The chalice could be poisoned.

Again, I had to try to make it clear that what I was attempting to speak about was 'Christian' holiness. I had no idea that Bishop Stephen Neill intended to make this the key adjective in his Carnahan lectures in 1958. I had rashly entertained some private hesitations about Wesley's 'scriptural' holiness because that adjective can cover such a wide range of meanings, particularly in the Old Testament. In much popular practice what has happened is that a biblical word which, in certain settings, had no more than a ritual or ceremonial significance or, in others, meant no more than 'belonging to' or 'for the sole use of', though in others—such as the writings of the later prophets—carried a strongly ethical requirement, has been filled, irrespective of its original context, with all the fullness of Christ. It can be argued that this is of little consequence so long as the end result is preached—and this is indeed what our Brengle did. Avoiding the slow biblical enrichment of the word, he came forthrightly to his final conclusion that 'there is no such thing as holiness apart from "Christ in you".' But this firmly secured the word to its New Testament foundation and, so long as holiness is equated with growth in Christlikeness, no seeker will go far astray.

It was some time later when, with the delight of a watcher

when some new planet swims into his ken, I discovered what C. H. Dodd had written on this very point.

> To place the idea of the Holy at the centre of ethics has certain dangers. It may easily throw the conception of right and wrong over to the side of the irrational, and set up a system of superstitious fears and taboos. The Pharisaism in which Paul had been bred did not wholly avoid a taint of the irrational in its ethical code. It proscribed certain foods, for example, because of an obscure sense that they were 'unholy' or 'unclean', just as it proscribed murder and adultery.
>
> Paul was saved from this chiefly because he identified the 'spirit of holiness' with the 'spirit of Christ', and so had a ready point of reference in a Figure standing in the clear light of history, with the concrete solidity of a powerful human personality; and One whose morality in word and deed was reasonable and humane, with no taint of taboo in His ideal of holiness.
>
> We may fairly say that it is never safe to emphasise the call to holiness as part of Christian teaching, unless the idea of the Holy is understood by constant reference to the Jesus of the gospels, His example and teaching.*

Here was theological rock beneath my feet. The gifts of the Spirit are the virtues of Jesus and the virtues of Jesus are the gifts of the Spirit. No 'baptism of the Spirit' can 'improve' on Jesus. Our highest spiritual goal—and what a goal it is!—is to be increasingly conformed to His image. Thus my apprehensions were less acute when in 1953, as Principal of the International (William Booth Memorial) Training College, I found myself responsible for the weekly Thursday evening holiness meetings at Camberwell.

Dr. Barclay has described sanctification as a lost article of the Christian faith but, whatever the errors of expression and explanation made by some well-intentioned exponents

*'The Epistle to the Romans', *Moffatt New Testament Commentary* (Hodder & Stoughton), p. 191.

of the doctrine, the Army continues to proclaim the will of God for His people to be their sanctification. Regular weekly holiness meetings go back to 1879 when the twenty-three-year-old Bramwell Booth commenced them in Whitechapel in a room seating seventy people. To this date every corps has its weekly holiness meeting on a Sunday morning, and most divisions a weeknight holiness meeting at some central point. Those associated with the International Training College have long been among the best attended of all. In *The House of my Pilgrimage* General Orsborn has described the slightly built but magnetic figure of Thomas McKie who led these gatherings in pre-First World War days. When between the wars the training college was rebuilt at Denmark Hill and Commissioner Samuel Hurren appointed Principal, that ardent South Londoner resolved that Camberwell should be a second Congress Hall on the Surrey side of the river—even to the shape and seating of the building.

During the Second World War the Camberwell hall was damaged and the Thursday night meetings had to be suspended. But with the coming of peace the weekly meeting wonderfully revived, and I was given what I had not enjoyed since the thirties on the Clydeside—a regular congregation, though one much larger than any entrusted to me before. Here each week from the middle of August to late December, and again from early January to the middle of May, was an opportunity to lead the public worship of The Salvation Army in that unforced blend of reverent gladness and ordered freedom which can lift a congregation to sit in heavenly places. The singing of the women's voices was an unfailing joy. The personal testimonies of the cadets were largely free from pious jargon. Their spontaneous responses warmed a leader's heart. And to speak of that work of divine grace known as sanctification as the unfolding of Christ's own character in the life of the believer was a privilege for which many a man more qualified than myself would have given his right hand. I never felt able to announce in advance that what the congregation was about to hear was a message from the Spirit Himself, for at times my mind would fear whether my heart truly meant what I was actually saying. No less than any other man a preacher has to remember the gospel saying that by his words he can be condemned. Indeed, the risk is greater for him for he utters so many more of them than most of his fellows. If, however, in the goodness and mercy of God, his is a genuine word of the Lord, then that fact will be self-evident. If it is not, then no label personally affixed can hide the unwelcome truth. Far better to make no attempt either to con the congregation or to deceive oneself.

The pastoral side of a Principal's work was as demanding— and rewarding—as his public work. The cadets were his flock and the sheep of his pasture. He met them as a body twice or thrice each week. He talked with everyone of them person- ally during the session. He campaigned with them in small groups in London and the provinces. This soon developed into a two-way traffic. As Anna sings in the musical in which she is linked with the king of Siam: 'If you become a teacher, by your pupils you'll be taught.' While the officers appointed to the Men's and Women's Sides served their charges with jealous care, there were sundry occasions when the standards required of an officer-to-be had to be maintained. Then I was grateful that when Anne Ross Cousin wrote—

> With mercy and with judgment
> My web of time He wove—

mercy came first. To terminate the cadetship of any lad or girl was no joy. If the individual concerned thought that he (or she) had failed, no less did the Principal. This was the very last resort, agreed only when there was no other possible option.

Some reader may regard this chapter as incomplete because so far there are no references to the writer's own spiritual disciplines. This is not by accident. By taking thought a man can cultivate some kind of public image, but anyone who tries to put a face on the work of the Spirit is condemned in advance. 'Be careful not to make a show of your religion,' said Jesus. It is notoriously difficult to judge a man's personal holiness by his public bearing. He may preach like an angel and yet be an impossible colleague or a difficult husband. Nor is it always easy to know whether he is, or is not, pushing his own barrow under the guise of his vocation. He may not even know himself. On the other hand, he may—and take still more pains to conceal the truth.

One thing is certain—the closer walk with God of which William Cowper wrote is not marked by any increasing sense of self-assured goodness, but by a deeper awareness of the infection of sin. This is not, like beauty, skin deep; it gets into the bloodstream. That is why the greatest saints have always been the greatest penitents. Why, for example, the ageing William Booth could write to his grown-up children: 'My great sorrow is that I have loved the Lord so imperfectly.' A clever man may think he knows how clever he is, but a good man does not know how good he is. His eye is not turned inward upon any self-induced image but outward and upward to his Lord.

Moses 'did not know that . . . his face shone because he had been speaking to the Lord' (Exodus 34:29, N.E.B.)—but those who saw him knew. Personal holiness has no need to advertise itself. Indeed, it had better not—lest what began as personal should end by becoming professional. Rarely does a happily married couple speak of their personal intimacies. It is the philanderer who boasts of his conquests and is ready to advise all and sundry of the ploys to which he resorts to gain his dubious ends. But the contentedness of a husband and wife is rooted in a mutual commitment which speaks for itself. They have no need continually to refer to what is plainly self-evident. And the believer who has committed himself to his Lord, and who maintains that commitment, is even more content. He knows himself to be compassed about by a love in which there is no variableness. 'I nestle down in His will', one saint used to say when the wind was unpleasantly high. The divine-human relationship is not one of the schoolroom where the textbook is king, but of the family where unspoken affection and mutual understanding go hand in hand.

All in all it would be hard to improve upon Catherine

Booth's earlier description of sanctification as 'the simple reception of Christ as an all sufficient Saviour, dwelling in my heart and thus cleansing it from all sin.' If we have once made Him welcome then, with our continued consent, He can be trusted to complete the good work which He has begun so that 'when He shall appear, we shall be like Him'.

6

Many Things to Write

I HAVE RARELY found much reading a weariness to the flesh— but this was an old man's observation and one can only pray that such a fate may long be delayed. What is true is that my early range of reading was circumscribed—circumscribed for one thing by the climate of the Movement in which I was reared. In *A Goodly Heritage* General Wilfred Kitching has related how *The Home Pianoforte Tutor*—in which, apart from the preliminary exercises and scales, all the tunes were either hymns or Salvation Army songs—was deemed to be the only proper manual for his early musical instruction. Both he and his teacher hoped for richer pastures in future days, but the boy was then given a bound volume of *The Musical Salvationist* for 1904 as the basis for further tuition.

A similar situation existed with regard to reading. In 1884 William Booth had published a volume of more than 250 pages entitled *The Training of Children*, dealing—among other things—with dress, education, companionships, strong drink, smoking, amusements and reading. The Bible was given first place as required reading. William Booth's own household was founded on the Bible. 'The one unquestioned and unquestionable centre of their life,' so wrote his official biographer, 'was . . . the Bible as the Word of God.' Before any superior eyebrows are raised, might not this be preferable to the more general ignorance of our own day? In a recent

66

'Brain of Britain' contest, a group of adults could not say who was Abraham's wife. Hagar was the nearest guess.

After the Bible came Salvation Army books and periodicals, along with history, biography, travel and the natural sciences. But fiction was out. Members of The Christian Mission undertook neither to read nor sell *The London Journal* or *The Family Herald*. And fairy tales were out as well. 'We should distinctly forbid . . . "Jack and the beanstalk".' As for 'novels or love stories', these 'should be kept from children as you would rank poison'. Bramwell Booth has written that his mother took 'an extreme view about fiction . . . nor did she give her children fiction to read'. It must be added that not all her household shared her extreme views. Begbie has referred to William Booth's fondness for *Jane Eyre* and *Les Misérables*, as well as for the historical romances of Sir Walter Scott to which he turned in middle life. His eldest son, however, read fiction only when on holiday. Every man with much to do has to be selective.

But for the generation to which my dedicated parents belonged what the Founder said was next to the oracles of God, and reinforced their understandable desire to protect their two boys from the corruption of this present world. I was seriously taken to task when discovered engrossed in *The Three Musketeers*. Milady was not at all to my mother's liking. Of course, much of the incident flowed over a young boy's head and I submitted to the loss of Dumas without really understanding why. I was less able to comprehend why *The Magnet* and *The Gem* should be placed on the index. I would not have contended for Sexton Blake and his dog Pedro. Their particular calling did take them at times into unsavoury surroundings. But Harry Wharton and company always played with the straightest of straight bats. They were no less on the side of the angels than the characters in *Fenella's Fetters* or *Jolly the Joker* which appeared on the annual prize list for those who had secured 104 marks out of 104 for regular attendance and good conduct at the two principal children's meetings held on each Sunday throughout the year. At Greyfriars virtue was always triumphant. The cad was invariably laid low. What was more bewildering about this fiat was that

I knew from the works of the Methodist minister brothers, Silas and Joseph Hocking, available on the family bookshelf, that the righteous could be pressed above measure. One of my early memories is of reading, while the household was out and by the light and warmth of a coal fire, *The Strange Adventures of Israel Pendray*, a Cornish preacher who, unwittingly staying overnight at an inn of evil repute, narrowly escaped death by quitting his bed just before some contraption, designed to suffocate him as he slept, was lowered from the ceiling of his room by some noiseless mechanism operated by an unseen hand.

But one's general reading was circumscribed at its source as well. Junior libraries were virtually unknown. No school I ever attended had a library of its own. Nor was the open access system in operation, not in pre-First World War days even in a city like Glasgow. Libraries were not for browsing. The would-be borrower never saw the book on which his heart was set until it was formally handed to him by the librarian or his assistant. The standard procedure was to consult the catalogue to discover if the required volume was actually listed. If so, noting the five or six figure number against the title, the hopeful borrower would consult what resembled a giant train indicator. If the book was 'in', a small oblong shape bearing the required number would show white. If 'out', the oblong would be black—and the process would have to start all over again from scratch. However, the white signal meant that one could now approach the library assistant half hidden behind what looked like a ticket office window in a Victorian station booking hall. But if the book passed out was not what had been anticipated—a not infrequent happening with small boys whose choices were at times random—the only option was to keep it. Books once borrowed could not be exchanged until the following day. The wonder is that books were borrowed at all—but youngsters can have an insatiable thirst.

The First World War did not encourage reading. I carried no volume of minor English poets in my kitbag. Thought was at a discount. "You're not paid to think,' an N.C.O. of the old school bellowed at me when I prefaced my hesitant apology for misunderstanding an order with 'I thought that . . .' In any case, how could one read after dark in a tent? Or even in a billet? 'Lights out!' was decreed by a voice other than one's own. Nor was the fellowship of the canteen marked by any distinctively intellectual overtones. The majority opinion was that any individual gift should be employed for the common pleasure. In other words, the piano stool was the expected place of duty for any man who could so much as pick out a tune with one finger.

Within a year of demobilisation, however, I was a Salvation Army officer, albeit with the most junior probationary rank. Whatever can be said against the twenties, bliss was it then to be alive, especially for the ex-serviceman. Whatever may be the official view, his true feelings were expressed in the uninhibited vernacular of his marching songs.

When this dreadful* war is over,
No more soldiering for me . . .

The twenties were good years for The Salvation Army. If the work had succumbed to the ideological pressures of the revolution in Russia, new openings were made in Austria, Bolivia, Brazil, Ghana, Kenya, Nigeria and Zambia (then Northern Rhodesia). It is true that the Movement undeniably suffered from the convulsion of 1929, but the work continued thanks to the faithfulness of the rank and file. Nowadays it is fashionable in certain quarters to bestow but faint praise upon church life and thought between the wars, but were church congregations as large today as they were then, we might think that the Kingdom was at hand. This was true virtually across the board. Leading preachers still filled the leading churches. In the twenties a Studdert Kennedy could stump the country and fill the largest public halls unaided. What he would have done with a Billy Graham organisation behind him is more than can be imagined—except that he would not have been Studdert Kennedy. A less spectacular

*Or stronger adjective according to personal taste.

but equally (or even more?) effective ministry was being carried on by Canon Peter Green at St. Philip's, Salford. Begun in 1911, it continued until 1936—twenty-five years. But across the way in Ancoats the Star Hall had been handed over to The Salvation Army and the preaching of salvation and holiness—Frank Crossley's twin themes—continued as before.

Indeed, the Army in Britain took large congregations for granted. Brighton, Bristol, Norwich, Oldham, Plymouth, Sheffield—to name half-a-dozen centres at random—were areas where Sunday evening congregations approached, and not infrequently reached, four figures. One domestic joke of this period told of a band whose numbers were so large that every man did not always know his neighbour. 'Haven't I seen you before?' said one such to another as they met on annual holiday. 'You may have done,' was the reply, 'I play in 'X' band.' 'I thought so', was the triumphant rejoinder. 'I play in that band myself!'

At the same time, General Orsborn's dictum that the Army did not consist of a small number of large corps but a large number of small corps was probably more accurate. During the twenties some of these witnessed scenes of spiritual awakening when men and women without any church affiliation whatever were truly converted unto God. I was a minor participant on some of these occasions. Just before closing time a small group of Salvationists—often no more than half-a-dozen—would station themselves strategically near to a well-patronised public house in the town and begin to sing two or three well-known hymns. Those emerging at the cry: 'Time, gentlemen, please', would often join in. A suggestion would be made that the Army hall was not far away and the choice of favourite hymns could be continued indoors. Still singing, the company would proceed in orderly disorder as far as the hall and, once inside, the proceedings would continue in the same unorthodox fashion. What was virtually essential was an organist or pianist whose knowledge of popular hymnology was truly catholic and who, like Paderewski on his baby grand, could 'play in any old key'. My time in service canteens had not been wasted. And if a miner, followed by his whippet, came to the Mercy Seat, the place of prayer, that secular apprenticeship acquired a new and sacred value.

These years of spiritual development were years of intellectual enlightenment as well. It dawned on me that, in the service of God, there was no necessary incompatibility between head and heart.

Nowadays, when translations of the Bible into the common tongue follow hard on one another's heels, it is not easy to recapture the impact of James Moffatt's translation of the New Testament in 1915, of the Old Testament in 1924, and of the publication of both together in 1926. F. F. Bruce commented more recently: 'If a translator's business is to produce on his hearers the same effect as the original text produced on those who read or heard it, Moffatt succeeded wonderfully.' My own parallel edition of the Moffatt New Testament dated 1922 is still on my shelves.

(Those shelves had the most modest of beginnings. As I had no fixed abiding place they had to be (a) collapsible and (b) portable. A working joiner in a town where I was stationed provided me with a set, stained and varnished, complete with screws, for one pound sterling. They remained in my service for more than twenty years).

But Moffatt's was not the first of the so-called modern translations to command attention. Ante-dating my Moffatt by nearly twenty years is my father's copy of *The Twentieth Century New Testament* presented to him—and to all who attended with him—at the officers' councils conducted in 1905 by Bramwell Booth, then the Chief of the Staff. So highly was this translation appreciated that a special edition was printed bearing the Army's name.

To my limited but slowly awakening mind the church was intellectually alive as well, though this judgment may have been due to the fact that it was I who was coming alive. This was not the work of one particular school of thought. T. R. Glover first produced his *Jesus of History* in 1917, of which there were nineteen reprints in the next ten years, but Charles Gore also brought out his *Reconstruction of Belief* between 1921 and 1924. H. H. Farmer published his *Things Not Seen* in 1927, which Leslie Weatherhead described as 'the best volume of sermons I have ever read'—though at that time of day there must have been numerous other claimants for that honour. J. H. Jowett's *The Passion for Souls* was required reading for an evangelical and, as one of that school, John G. McKenzie was already exploring the borderlands which lie between mind and spirit.

For my part, I held my bucket at springs both sacred and secular—though the last adjective is inappropriate when applied to *The Manchester Guardian*, for with C. P. Scott his paper was his religion—as it was with other discerning spirits. In 'A parson's log'—an established weekly feature in *The Methodist Recorder* in the thirties—George Jackson once described how he met Principal Alexander Martin—a man not given to saying it with flowers—in Princes Street, Edinburgh. The conversation turned to *The Manchester Guardian*. 'The greatest Christian institution in the land,' commented the Principal, 'not excluding the churches'. In those days the 'M.G.' could be obtained at half-price by certain professional people, including students and ministers of religion. I deemed myself to qualify for this bounty under one, or both, of these headings. In what other newspaper could prose daily be read written by masters of prose. Certainly nowhere else appeared both H. W. Nevinson and Neville Cardus, J. L. Hammond and Alfred Noyes, C. F. Andrews and Canon Peter Green, R. H. Tawney and C. E. Montague. The studiously burnished prose of Montague held me in thrall. His *Writer's Notes on his Trade* which appeared posthumously in 1930 became almost my second bible and, after bursting into print in 1925, the resultant style (save the mark!) was obviously Montague and water. This attitudinising which required that every other sentence should echo some turn of phrase culled from the more recondite reaches of English literature was a green-sickness from which, mercifully, I soon recovered. For one thing, I couldn't keep it up! In due course I learned the more excellent way of using the plainest of words in the most straightforward order in the shortest of sentences. Frills and furbelows were out.

This was just as well for from 1937 to 1947 I was charged (as earlier mentioned) with the down to earth task of preparing scripture teaching material for the youth and children's work of the Army. For each Sunday of the year three versions of the selected lesson material had to be made ready. One of these appeared in *The Young Soldier*, a children's paper with a weekly circulation in Britain of around a quarter of a million copies, written for children to be read by children. The official teaching manual contained the other two approaches—one designed for the company guard (or Sunday school teacher) upon which he could base his own presentation; the other was a more developed treatment for Bible classes. The war imposed its own paper rationing restrictions, reducing the manual from a pre-war 292 pages to a post-war 168. Smaller typefaces and fewer words were the order of the day—a discipline which possibly benefited the compiler most of all. These ten years meant a continual casting of one's bread upon the waters, but by no stranger waters did it fall than the Pacific internment camp where Leonard Woodward, a missionary officer who had been serving in the Celebes and who, with several hundred Roman Catholic and Protestant clergy, was held prisoner by the Japanese from 1942 to 1945. The weekly Bible class led by the Colonel was based on this textbook. During this time I was also required to prepare study material for corps cadets—the name given to young people, who by means of weekly evangelical studies and activities, seek to prepare themselves for the demands of Salvation Army soldiership and local officership.

Throughout these formative years I had the immense good fortune to serve under the then Colonel S. C. Gauntlett, Literary Secretary to General G. L. Carpenter, who himself had previously served in that capacity to General Bramwell Booth. One of the Colonel's many pen names was 'Bibliophile', which explains itself, and all his love of the Army's past, combined with his current wide-ranging European experience, was directed to acquaint the young people of the Army with the story of the Army.

Of course the war was still on. '101' had been all but de-

stroyed in the raid of May 10th/11th, 1941, and both Editorial
and Literary Departments were transferred to a derelict three-
story building which abutted on to the old headquarters and
was numbered 224, Upper Thames Street. Anything less like
the offices of a group of papers with a weekly circulation of more
than half-a-million could not be imagined. But this was the
setting where Bibliophile told me that the General had sanc-
tioned a new book programme aimed at Salvationist youth. I
had a shrewd idea who had inspired the programme in the
first place but had no idea that I was to be asked to undertake
the first in the series. But by October, 1942, *Salute to a Mill
Girl*, a pocket biography of Brigadier Martha Chippendale,
M.B.E., was off the press. Scores of titles followed over the
next twenty years. 15,000 copies of the *Salute* were sold, which
I followed with *He Had No Revolver* (the story of Edwin
Sheard and the criminal colony in the Andamans), *Down in
Demarara* (11,000 copies) and *The First Salvationist*—a brief
biography of William Booth which is still selling. Not without
reason did General Carpenter send his Literary Secretary a
handwritten note which ran:

> With regard to publishing, while my keen interest is
> behind a progressive programme, I gratefully acknowledge
> the vision of the framer of the programme, your own good
> self.

It was at this time while, with the rest of the country, the
Army had all its work cut out to cope with the present, that
negotiations were opened to find a publisher for a definitive
and detailed account of the Army's past. In 1950 I prepared
the blurb for the dust jacket of volume two, little dreaming
that twenty years later I would be writing volume six. Before
that, however, the Lutterworth Press published in 1944 a
primer of Old Testament study entitled *The Timeless Prophets*,
and the following year Collins brought out a set of children's
stories (ancient and modern) entitled *Half Hours With Heroes*.
The Bannisdale Press followed this up with a companion
volume in 1951. Two short biographies told the story of Albert

Moss, a Salvation Army officer whose cricketing fame is noted in Wisden, and also of my younger brother, a dedicated local officer in the Warrington (Lancs.) corps who was promoted to Glory while still in his thirties. Another appropriate publication during wartime was *The battle and the breeze*— an account of the work of the Army with the Forces from 1894 to date. I was also privileged at this time to speak at the weekly midday service held at The Campfield Press, the Army's printing house at St. Albans. Two of these sets of talks—*In the dinner hour* (which dealt with the ten commandments) and *Our Father* (based on the Lord's prayer) appeared in 1946 and 1948 respectively. Three study books for young people—*The Kingdom of God, The Salvationist and his Leisure* and *Jesus and Our Need* were published in 1951, 1954 and 1956 respectively.

But before that, in December, 1946, I was appointed to succeed my mentor, Bibliophile, as editor of *The Officer*, then called *The Officer's Review*. This magazine, circulating among all officers who understood English, first appeared in January, 1893, and like any other paper rose and fell with its editor. This is one of the inexorable laws of journalism. Under my predecessor not even wartime paper rationing, reducing the number of pages from ninety-six for a bi-monthly to sixty-four for a quarterly, had reduced the quality of those pages. Under his editorship the index of contributors read like the roll call of many nations—Ah Kow, Albro, Atkinson . . . Brash, Breien, Bruckner . . . Hein, Hellqvist, Holbrook . . . Mabee, Marpurg, Muthiah . . . van der Werken, von Tavel, Westergaard. An international anthology brought to readers original poems by Salvationists in Dutch, French, German, Spanish and Swedish. An annual volume would contain studies of the life and work of such diverse characters as Nathan Söderblom, Tommy Fallot, Carl Hilty and Friedrich von Bodelschwingh.

From the beginning William Booth had determined that his new magazine should lift the sights of his officers, and he himself started the good work by contributing a series on 'How to preach'. Various homiletical aids were a regular feature and,

by the turn of the century, a 'Union for Bible Study' was
operating through its pages. The synoptic problem was
discussed. Within twelve months of W. M. Ramsay's travels in
Asia Minor, *The Officer* was quoting his discovery near Lystra
of the Greek inscription bearing on Acts 14:12. The teaching
of the book of Jonah was described as of 'equal rank' with that
of the great 'Seer of the Exile' (Isaiah 40 ff.) and lit with 'the
morning air of high day which shines upon the parables of
Jesus'. 'The servant of the Lord' in the Servant Songs was
held to be 'sometimes Israel as a whole (42:19), sometimes the
faithful or true Israel (44:1, 2, 21), rising in 52:13 and 53:12
into a Person who makes atonement for His people and brings
in the final glory'. Plainly the Army of that day was not wholly
staffed by theological illiterates. If some of our fathers in the
faith were, in the apostolic sense, 'unlearned and ignorant men'
they were also, in the same apostolic sense, 'full of wisdom and
the Holy Ghost'.

In the footsteps of past editors I had to plant my own.
An international Army had to continue to be encouraged to
know the Army. So the last complete year of this assignment
carried a factual appreciation of the Army's work in Scotland
and Ireland, in Malaysia and in Denmark. Unpublicised
aspects of service—such as the Fire Insurance Corporation,
the Chaplain's department of the Men's Social Services, the
Children's Aid department of the Women's Social Services
and the Reliance Bank—were given authoritative treatment.
Studies of the current problems of juvenile delinquency in
Australia, Britain, Germany, Sweden and the United States
respectively were provided by officers stationed in those
countries. New Army publications included *En Herrgardsfroken
i uniform* (a biography of Hedwig von Haartman in Swedish)
and *Ainsi sont nés nos cantiques* (a study of the hymns of the
evangelical movement in France by Lieut.-Commissioner
Gustave Isely). Upwards of two hundred other books were
reviewed throughout the year, embracing such diverse authors
as Geoffrey Nuttall and Peter Marshall, Norman Snaith and
Campbell Morgan.

One private scoop was the publication of selected extracts

from the prison diary of Lieut.-Colonel Leonard Woodward. The Colonel hid his diary which, as an additional precaution, he wrote in Oema, the language of the Toradjas among whom he had been working, sometimes in a length of bamboo, sometimes under a heap of stones, and sometimes sewn into the seat of his trousers. To keep any kind of record was a punishable offence and, as no other internee had done so, this document was of unique value.

The four years as Principal of the International Training College gave time only to complete *Portrait of a Salvationist* (a biography of Bibliophile himself), and to prepare for the press *The call to holiness* which was based on a selection of Thursday evening addresses given at Camberwell. The years in Australia, 1957–1963, as with the period as General from 1963–1969, gave little leisure for writing save the occasional article but, thanks to the understanding of my successor, General Erik Wickberg, retirement brought new opportunities. At his suggestion a further volume was added to the history of the Army, covering the years between the outbreak of the First World War and the conclusion of the second. Then the success of *The Soldier's Armoury*, a book of daily Bible readings, persuaded Hodder and Stoughton to suggest an *Armoury* commentary based upon these studies which had begun in January, 1955. First hopes were that the whole of the New Testament might be covered in a single volume, but this would have resulted in a book of unmanageable size. So a commentary on the four gospels appeared in 1973 and a second volume, covering the epistles, was published in the autumn of 1975. As all I did was to select the requisite passages and arrange them as a congruous whole I feel free to express a judgment. Working my way through past issues of the *Armoury* it was a pleasant revelation to discover how little there was of pious padding and how frequently there occurred genuine insights into the relevance of the biblical text to the reader's daily life. No one involved in the preaching of the gospel—cadet, Lieutenant, Corps Cadet Guardian, Envoy, Band Sergeant—will fail to find in the *Armoury* commentary some illustration, or suggested line of approach, or illuminating observation, wherewith to prime the pump when the mental temperature is below zero.

One other piece of written work provided a good deal of pleasure—the one-volume history of the Army, again published by Hodder and Stoughton in 1975 at the agreeable price of 75p and entitled *No Discharge in This War*. This was planned as an interpretation of the spirit and work of the Army against a twentieth-century background, though there were those who enquired whether this paperback was really necessary. Was not the work of the Army sufficiently publicised—even over-publicised—already? Experience compelled—and still compels—me to answer no.

For one thing, the Christian faith—from which the Army derives its past origin and its present motivation—has to be told afresh to each successive generation. The basic facts of that faith remain the same but the manner of their presentation has to take into account the changing character of the audience. Even the blessed apostle Paul suited his argument and his allusions to his various hearers. No one is disloyal to the gospel because he remembers the year and the context in which he and his listeners are living.

In the second place, the public memory is short. Time itself sees to that. To have some first-hand adult memory of the beginning of the Second World War a man has now to be turned fifty. Simply as a domestic matter the Army has to retell the reasons for its birth and growth. The duty of keeping alive the significance of certain key events in the history of Israel rested upon the older generation (Joshua 4:21, 22). This writer falls into that age group.

More importantly, those who serve—or observe—have ever to be reminded of what makes the Army tick. Judgments should not be formed merely upon what the eye sees. Of course the uniform is one of the Army's great assets. Without a word it declares that the wearer is at the service of anyone in need, whatever that need may be. For my own part, I can rarely walk down Ludgate Hill or along Cheapside without being stopped by some enquirer. And if it be said that most of these are foreigners, wanting to find their way around, I shall agree.

Even 'foreigners' know what the Army uniform stands for. At least it does not represent an insular Anglo-Saxon institution.

Every good has its dangers. It is easy to see no further than the attractive face of an Army girl framed in her becoming bonnet. As one man-about-town enquired in astonishment at an Army meeting where I was present: 'Where do all these good-looking girls come from?' The media knows on whom to train their cameras. What can be overlooked is that the willingness to serve shown by those who wear what Bishop Oxnam (at the Evanston Assembly of the World Council of Churches) called 'the simple, significant uniform of the Salvationist' arises out of their personal religion. They are first and foremost committed Christians. Their works are an outcome of their faith. It cannot be denied that they live by standards which even some other believers call puritan. That could be the reason for their unforced happiness. Certainly they believe in chastity before marriage and fidelity thereafter, and regard the family home not as an adaptable social convenience but of divine ordinance. These convictions—dismissed by some as outmoded—are shared by men and women Salvationists alike who are drawn not just from a small white western island society but from all five continents and from many races of many colours. Their common loyalty to Christ overrides their diverse backgrounds. They believe the announced purpose of God to be that men shall come from the east and the west and the north and the south to sit down and eat bread in His kingdom. For this reason they are one in spirit and purpose with all who pray: Thy kingdom come.

7

A Land Thou Knowest Not

IN THE LATE spring of 1957 I was summoned to the General's office at International Headquarters—at this time still at Denmark Hill—to be told that I was to be appointed to the leadership of the Eastern Australia territory, with headquarters in Sydney and covering New South Wales, Queensland and the Australian Capital Territory, with Papua New Guinea thrown in for good measure.

'Speak to your wife about it and see me again in the morning,' said the General but, as I had already spent nearly forty years going where I was told, it was rather late in the day to alter the habit of obedience. My wife and I had no hesitation on our own account; all that concerned us was to see our children provided for—always the principal anxiety of officer-parents appointed overseas. However, this was not difficult as our two elder daughters were already happily married. John had taken his degree with first-class honours at Oxford and, having almost completed his two years of national service, was to enter the training college the week after our departure. We decided that our youngest daughter, Elizabeth, had better come with us. She was sixteen years of age and still at school. Changes in schooling can at times hinder the education of some officers' children. Happily not so with Elizabeth for, like the other three, she went on to take her degree at the University of Sydney.

In those days the Suez Canal was open so we pursued a

measured course via Gibraltar, Naples, Port Said, Aden, Colombo and Freemantle—where leisure ended. We docked just after seven o'clock in the morning, were greeted by the officers and band of the Freemantle corps, and that day shared in three public meetings—at Perth Fortress, Maylands and Leederville—before sailing again at five in the afternoon. We reached Sydney at nine o'clock on Friday morning and were paying our respects to the Governor General, Field Marshal Sir William Slim, at four o'clock the same afternoon.

Plainly our business now required haste. On the Saturday evening we made our bow in the Sydney Congress Hall— that most delightful of Salvation Army meeting places where, thanks to the generous curve of the gallery, the entire congregation can be comfortably at one with the speaker and he with them. This remains one of my favourite Salvation Army halls. Three meetings on the Sunday were followed by an introduction to departmental heads on the Monday at 10 a.m., to the entire headquarters staff at 2.30 p.m. and to the staff and cadets at the training college at 5 p.m. Wednesday took us to Canberra and, in the interests of the work in Papua New Guinea, to call upon Mr. Paul Hasluck, then the Minister for Territories. On Thursday, after a civic reception by the Lord Mayor of Sydney, we left by evening train for Brisbane. Then followed a weekend's round of engagements in the Queensland state capital, an early morning departure by plane on the Tuesday for Rockhampton—with three meetings during the day, and yet another flight the next morning to Townsville—though this time with only two meetings, after which we retraced the twelve hundred and fifty miles to Sydney.

Those first weeks taught me much—not least the unique position which the Army held throughout the country. Gore and Saunders, our founding fathers in the Commonwealth, held their first meeting in the Botanic Gardens, Adelaide, on September 5th, 1880—the year in which Ned Kelly, the last of the bush-rangers, was captured and executed. So the Army has grown up with Australia from the days of the wild colonial boys to the present sophistications of Sydney's Kings Cross.

It is therefore no recent importation but is deeply rooted in the soil of the land which it seeks to serve.

In the second place, the Australian is aware how much he owes—and continues to owe—to the Army, both in war and peace. God forbid that any society should profit—even in goodwill—from the two world wars of the twentieth century, but the names of William McKenzie and Arthur McIlveen are representative of many whose selfless service with the armed forces of the Commonwealth is still remembered. The former shared the ordeal of the Dardanelles; the latter the siege of Tobruk. Sir Arthur's (for he was the first Salvation Army officer to be knighted) 'secret weapon'—his portable gramophone—has its place of honour in the Australian War Memorial at Canberra. Nor does the Army rest on its laurels in peace time. When Cyclone Tracy struck Darwin in the early hours of Christmas morning, 1974, an initial meeting to formulate emergency plans was held in Melbourne in the evening and Commissioner H. J. Warren left for Darwin the following morning, arriving on the second civilian plane to reach the airport with news that massive relief in money and in kind was on its way.

Early proof of the regard in which the Army is held came my way when, with my youngest daughter, I attended a reception given in Sydney in September, 1959, for Princess Alexandra who on this occasion was anxious to meet representative young people. She was being escorted by the Hon. J. J. Cahill, then Premier of New South Wales, when a small group of Labour members (by one of the inherited twists of state politics Roman Catholics almost to a man) thought that we were being neglected. 'Over here, Joe,' they called out to the Premier, motioning at the same time to the two of us who, with due English reserve, were trying to look as inconspicuous as possible. But 'over here' Joe and the Princess came. And the proprieties—Australian if not English—did not even blink.

This same attitude prevails at all levels of Commonwealth life—as is only to be expected when the father of the Rt. Hon. Sir Paul Hasluck, Governor General from 1969 to 1974, was the veteran Salvation Army officer, Major E'thel Hasluck. On one

of my earlier visits to the Federal Capital I was being shown
over the government buildings by Mr. A. V. Thompson, a
Salvationist who was Labour member for Port Adelaide, when
we were greeted by Dr. H. V. Evatt. Within minutes I was
being invited to take lunch with the Leader of the Federal
Opposition. In his office Dr. Evatt had a number of original
drawings by David Low, and we found common interest in
the fact that Low had begun his professional career by drawing
anti-gambling and anti-smoking cartoons for the New Zealand
War Cry. On his side Dr. Evatt had made some study of the
liberty of public assembly and regarded the stand which the
Army had taken in Britain in the nineteenth century to sustain
its outdoor religious meetings and marches—a position subsequently upheld by the High Court of the Queen's Bench
Division—as a valuable contribution to the right of lawful
assembly.

Some time later he told me that he would like to present a
cornet to the Army. It was agreed that this should be given to
our band at Canberra which, in Australian parlance, was
'battling' somewhat at that time, but that the presentation itself
would be in the Sydney Congress Hall on Saturday, July 26th,
1958. This gave the press a minor field day. How long had 'the
Doc.' been playing the cornet ? Would he oblige with a solo at
some point in the proceedings ? But our guest was too seasoned
a campaigner to be provoked by this small arms fire. Sometime
earlier he had purchased a Salvation Army tune book when
visiting our trade department in Melbourne, and now he told
the congregation his favourite hymn tune, which the Congress
Hall Band, under Bandmaster Harold Morgan, promptly
played. During the proceedings I wondered how long it would
take to get on the same terms with the Leader of the Opposition
at Westminster, no matter to which party he belonged.

This easy open-ended relationship prevails at the ground-
floor level as well. The Australian reaction to a stuffed shirt is
matched only by his willingness to accept any man on his
proven merit—as is borne out by the story of Jim Crocker who
spent all his adult life in Broken Hill, a town of some thirty
thousand people lying seven hundred miles west of Sydney and

possibly the most strongly unionised town in the world. On certain appointed days in the year every man wears his union badge to his place of employment. Crocker was a salvation soldier, i.e. a layman, belonging to one of the smallest religious groups in a town where the strongest church possessed a theology and structure differing at many points from his own faith and practice. He held the rank of Envoy—somewhat akin to the standing of a lay preacher—yet was possibly one of the best-known men in the place and, during his lifetime, had conducted the funeral of more than eight hundred men and women of every creed and of no creed at all. He was literally 'chaplain to the Barrier'.

When in May, 1960, I travelled to Broken Hill to attend the civic service held to mark his admission to the Order of the Founder (the highest honour the Army can bestow) there were only three of us in uniform on the platform—Jim Crocker, the corps officer at Broken Hill and myself. But we were surrounded by the Barrier Industrial Band to accompany the congregational singing, the Mayor and Council, along with the members of the Federal and State parliaments, the churches, the mammoth Broken Hill Pty., Ltd., the trade unions and the voluntary organisations of the city. A full-length portrait of William Booth looked down upon the crowded hall, though I may have been mistaken in thinking that I saw his eyes gleam approvingly when the Mayor declared: 'Jim is not a person; he is an institution.' Crocker's response was to give his personal testimony which was heard without any hint of dissent. Doubtless any other attitude would have been out of character in a town which was well aware of the way in which the Army, though few in number in their midst, could match any demand.

Earlier that year when a group of British trade unionists had been visiting Broken Hill, one of their number had unexpectedly been taken ill and died. The Barrier Industrial Council, on which sit both management and men, turned to the Army officer. Could Mr. Tom North's family in South Wales be advised of their bereavement? A cable was dispatched at 2.30 p.m. South Australian time; a reply was received by 9 a.m. South Australian time the following morning. The family had been visited, sympathy was expressed, prayer had been offered. 'It is such actions and kindly understanding,' wrote the Secretary of the Industrial Council to the corps officer, 'that has placed The Salvation Army so high in the esteem of the people of this city.'

This outlook is also shared by those who are involved in the nitty-gritty of public life—the police, for example. In Sydney we have long been fortunate in our police court officers. The work for women of Brigadier Pearl Mason (who was promoted to Glory on June 7th, 1958) was honoured not only by her Army comrades but by an act of remembrance in the Central Court, Sydney, which was shared by the magistracy, members of the legal profession and the general public. Her service was continued by Lieut.-Colonel Lily Sampson and, for men in need, there was Brigadier John Irwin who was always a friend indeed. The result of this was that our presence in the courts was positively welcomed and our relationship with the police could hardly have been improved upon. One public evidence of this was the arrangement made by Mr. Norman Allan, Commissioner for Police in New South Wales, for a parade and meeting for the police in the Sydney Congress Hall. I had more than once attended by invitation a police passing-out parade and now the Commissioner invited me to accompany him on his parade of inspection in Elizabeth Street. Truth to tell I had some inward hesitation. I still carried memories of being inspected to my no small discomfiture during the First World War. Happily this time no names were took! And so I had no hesitation about welcoming members of the Force who filled the Congress Hall from floor to ceiling; the police choir on the platform; the Petersham Band under Bandmaster Fred Gott an island of colour amid a sea of blue. The speakers chose themselves—Lily Sampson, John Irwin and Mr. Norman Allan.

Relationships with the churches were also very close—particularly in the evangelical diocese of Sydney. On Anzac Day the opportunity, and responsibility, of speaking in the Domain was shared between church leaders, Roman Catholic and Protestant alike. General Albert Orsborn was given this privilege when he visited Sydney in 1950. At Christmas time the presentation of the Bethlehem story in Hyde Park was again a co-operative effort between Roman Catholics, Anglicans and the Army. I also had the pleasure of knowing both the orthodox and the liberal Jewish rabbis, and if when in Brisbane I could not share Dean Baddeley's passion for the turf he was always stimulating company. My governing principle in public relations was that if the Army could further the cause of Christ by participating in public events, then participate we should. After all, the presence of thirty men marching with their characteristic Australian stride along George Street in the Waratah parade provided an ungainsayable testimony that their uprightness of bearing arose out of their uprightness of living. And the attendant rows of Australian girls in their uniform with their timbrels bore witness that what might otherwise be dismissed as plain goodness was uncommonly attractive.

These national festival days were not to be dismissed as purely secular efforts. That is all they would become if Christian people did not take part in them. But the sight of the flag, the discipline of the band, the unstudied appeal of the timbrellists, were all a living verification of the worth of the Christian faith. With not the least wish to do anyone out of a job, organisers of inter-church rallies in our western world should remember that there is no need to pay a high fee for the services of professional musicians when, as likely as not, there is a competent Salvation Army band in the neighbourhood whose members, while providing music of equal quality, will add the undeniable weight of their own personal Christian experience to the challenge of the occasion. Only ask for them in good time; they are in considerable demand.

The Graham crusades bring their own skilful accompanists but their choirs are recruited locally, as was the case when Dr. Graham came to Sydney in 1961. A number of our Sydneyside Salvationists sang in the choir, even laying aside their uniform—an unusual step—to do so. The Army was represented on the main co-ordinating committee by Lieut.-Colonel Reuel McClure, and a number of our women officers and employees from the territorial headquarters shared in the labour of the postal follow-up work. An analysis of those who came to the front at Dr. Graham's invitation is worth noting. Sixty-four per cent of the seekers came forward for what in our Army terminology is called salvation, and this was the word used in the official report. Thirty-seven per cent of the seekers were young teenagers—i.e. in the twelve to fourteen age group. Twenty-two per cent of those who came forward were nineteen years of age and over. Analysis by church affiliation showed that fifty-eight per cent belonged to the Church of England. A further twenty-three per cent had Presbyterian, Methodist or Congregational connections. The remaining nineteen per cent were divided among the Church of Christ, the Lutherans, the Brethren, with sundry Pentecostal groups and city missions and included twenty-two Roman Catholics. Two per cent of those who came forward declared themselves Salvationists. By and large both congregations and seekers were made up of those who already had some church connection, however tenuous, and undoubtedly church life was quickened. One interesting Salvation Army reaction was the expressed desire for more personal testimony and less waffle in our meetings. With both points I fully agreed. After all, if Brian Booth (then a test batsman of some distinction) could give his testimony in the place where he played cricket, could any bandsman hesitate to do the same either out of doors or in? For my part this revived a fellowship with Dr. Graham which had begun with his Harringay Crusade in 1954, was renewed at Earls Court in 1966 and again at Madison Square Gardens in New York in the summer of 1969.

Radio and television have also set before the Army in Australia an increasingly open door. The number of what in Britain are called commercial stations means that every town of any size has its local station whose manager welcomes with open arms anyone who has something to say and can say it. There is also the A.B.C.—the equivalent of the B.B.C. and modelled thereon—which provides nation-wide radio and television programmes. A number of our corps have long availed themselves of these media. To give two examples only, for many years the Sydney Congress Hall has had a transmitting room built into the senior hall—as has the Dulwich Hill Temple.

At the latter corps I found a willing and competent adviser in Wilbur Ford—a Salvationist technician who had a recording studio in his own home and under whose guidance I tried to improve my own untutored techniques.

Again, my approach to this matter was as direct as with any other opportunity. If a station offered five minutes, it was to be accepted, for that was the way to secure fifteen or twenty-five. No last-minute approach, even an obvious fill-in, was to be turned down. My aim was to make the quality of the present broadcast sufficiently attractive to secure consideration of its successor. Before long the Army was invited on several occasions to share in the 'Plain Christianity' series—a straightforward twenty-five minute approach to some aspect of the Christian faith and man's need of that faith. Thanks to the success of a previous telecast by Commissioner Edgar Grinsted, the A.B.C. agreed to televise for the first time an open-air meeting from the sea front at Manly on January 18th, 1959, in which the Sydney Congress Hall and the Territorial Singers took part. This group of women's voices had been formed by my distinguished predecessor and provided a further telecast at a peak viewing hour during Christmas, 1960.

In any of the state capitals this kind of work called for the highest technical standards; in the outback it could be more casual. In a country town whose name and that of the station will not be given, our forces, though faithful, were so meagre that to raise a band of four, including the two officers, was a major triumph. However, I ever kept in mind the previously quoted dictum of General Orsborn regarding small corps and prepared accordingly.

For this particular Sunday morning broadcast no script had been required, nor was there any hint of a balance and control test. About half an hour before we were due to go on the air a lad appeared, bearing a microphone, which he left on the table which stood in front of the platform and, paying out his cable, disappeared into the waiting van outside. Organ there was, but no organist. Swift action was needful. The organ was moved to a convenient angle close to the table. The four musicians were stationed towards the rear of the hall lest their accompaniment drown the voices of the faithful, but once the opening song was over they were bidden join in the congregational singing. I then announced the opening lines of each of the subsequent songs, moved smartly three paces to the right to the organ stool and played a few preliminary bars in the hope that some listener might think that a virtuoso of the highest order was presiding at the keyboard. To complete the illusion—or so I fondly hoped—I played while the offering was being received and, after the benediction, provided what I understand is called a postlude as we went off the air. Anyone who imagines that a Territorial Commander always has it served up to him on a plate has never been a Territorial Commander.

Perhaps the outstanding illustration of the developing work of the territory was the opening in Papua New Guinea, the second largest island in the world, an enterprise which has been largely financed by the Eastern Australia Territory itself. As far back as 1938 Commissioner Wm. R. Dalziel, the then Territorial Commander, had surveyed the island and recommended that Army work be commenced. At the time International Headquarters was unable to offer any financial aid, the Second World War broke out and the proposal lapsed. In 1949 International Headquarters revived the matter with Commissioner Joshua James but who felt, in his turn, that the territory could not undertake such a task singlehandedly.

In September, 1955, however, Commissioner Grinsted instructed Lieut.-Colonel Hubert Scotney, the then Field Secretary, accompanied by Senior-Captain George Carpenter, to make a fresh survey which reached out to cover New Britain as well as part of what is now West Irian. The upshot was that a territorial appeal was launched for £10,000 and Major and Mrs. Keith Baker were appointed to Port Moresby. The first Army meeting in Papua New Guinea was held on Sunday, October 21st, 1956, at the Kila Royal Constabulary Department where Major Baker met a Papuan lad called Kurau (or Kei) Geno. Kei became a Salvation Army recruit in January, 1957, and at the time of writing is the Captain who, with his wife, is stationed at Kokorogoro. The next Australian, Lieutenant Ian Cutmore, arrived in Port Moresby in November,

1956, and gave most valuable service for eleven years. Open-air work was commenced in February, 1957, and the first meeting for Europeans was held in the Boroko school in the following March. The opening meeting for the indigenous people living in Kaugere was held in the same month; a home league was begun in June; the first hall to be built was opened in Boroko in the October.

Commissioner and Mrs. Grinsted were then recalled to take charge of the British Territory and, as soon as a first round of the mainland divisions had been completed, I flew to Port Moresby in March, 1958. As is usual, there were both opportunities and adversaries. The administration warmly welcomed the Army. In a well-meant but misunderstood endeavour to encourage us, they gave it as their opinion that we would sweep the Island. We held no such high opinion of our powers, but understandably this prophecy did not endear the new arrivals on this heavily missionised island to those already engaged in the spread of the Christian faith. But the exacting conditions of probation laid down before a convert could become a recruit and a recruit a soldier, made it clear that we were not out to increase our numbers on the cheap but first to seek the spiritual and material good of the indigenous people—and so the agitation died away. The Assistant Administrator, Dr. J. Gunther, recognised this in his address at my first meeting:

... This country can progress only when it fully embraces Christianity, when the people have adopted Christian principles. There is need for education, but education must have as part of its curriculum the principles of Christ... There is a tremendous need for social welfare work, and Christian organisations are being asked to do more and more of this work on behalf of the government... The government has been proud to associate with you in developing a hostel in this town... We have made grants in aid ... and will continue to do so.

This was a generous enough charter and one result was that a mobile medical unit was purchased in Australia by the

Eastern Territory, shipped to Lae and then driven on its slow journey over unmade roads to Kainantu in the Eastern Highlands where Major Ruby Dalrymple and Lieutenant Dorothy Elphick set up their clinic. (Captain Elphick is in charge of the work in the Misapi area, though currently on sick leave.)

The hostel at Koki (a suburb of Port Moresby) to which the Assistant Administrator referred in his welcome speech, was opened in September, 1958. A weekly programme of meetings was commenced and adult education classes were also begun. In mid-1959 Major and Mrs. Baker concluded their pioneer term and were succeeded by Major and Mrs. Albert Smith. (The Major held the M.B.E., military division, for his services with the 2nd A.I.F.). Following up the plans of his predecessor, the new Regional Officer established a post at Koitaki in January, 1960, and in the same month a primary school was opened at Koki with a Salvationist head teacher. In the March of that year two Papuan cadets were welcomed at the training college at Sydney, but this experiment was not repeated. Early in 1961 work was commenced at Boregaina, and in September another hostel was opened at Lae—two hundred miles across the Owen Stanley Range. Initial capital costs were met by the administration but the running of the hostel was the responsibility and charge of the Army. In February, 1962, the training of indigenous cadets was regularised with Cadet and Mrs. Kei Geno and Cadet and Mrs. Kala Bogagu as the first admissions at Koki. Captain Geno's appointment has already been mentioned; Captain Bogagu is now Assistant to the Regional Commander.

A further new opening was at Kokorogoro, some five hours' walk on from Boregaina and, before my own term in Australia ended, Major and Mrs. Arthur Walz succeeded Major and Mrs. Smith. The work in Papua New Guinea has gone on from strength to strength. Half the officer personnel is indigenous so, despite current political changes, the place of the Army in the life of the people is assured.

Two other matters should be mentioned in this chapter, one of which is the recurring inspiration of the annual state congresses. The neighbouring Southern Territory enjoys four of these—in Melbourne, Adelaide, Perth and Hobart. The Eastern has to be content with two—in Sydney and Brisbane, but each usually lasts from Thursday afternoon over the weekend to Tuesday evening and unites all that is best in past and present Salvationist practice. For example, in each of the six congresses from 1957 to 1963 there was an all night of prayer. Sunday morning and evening were given over to the traditional themes of holiness and salvation. One weeknight was devoted to music and song and another to a youth programme. The Friday and the whole of the final Tuesday were occupied with officers' councils which were not exercises in self-congratulation but in self-examination. One year we had Commissioner Herbert Lord, whose Korean experiences were still fresh in the public mind, as our principal visitor; another year Commissioner Joseph Dahya—an outstanding Indian leader—was our guest. In 1960 the Chief of the Staff and Mrs. Commissioner Dray were our leaders; in 1963 General and Mrs. Kitching. These territorial congresses also allowed my wife and me to visit New Zealand in 1959 and in 1962 to travel to Melbourne.

The other event was that on the night of June 16th/17th, 1963, my wife was stricken without warning with transverse myelitis. On the Sunday she had shared in the leadership of young people's councils in the Petersham town hall, and her last public act on that day had been to offer prayer in the evening session for the young people present. On the following morning I discovered that she was paralysed from the waist down. Part of my immediate dilemma was that we were booked to sail in ten days' time for Great Britain where I had been summoned to take part in the election of a successor to General Wilfred Kitching, and it had been agreed that she could accompany me at our own charge. She was also understandably anxious to see her children again from whom she had been parted since the autumn of 1957. But the urgent necessity was an enquiry into the cause of the illness and treatment for the cure.

Dr. Herb Smartt, as compassionate a Salvationist as I have known, came at once to my help with professional advice. Next day my wife was in hospital and then began the long haul back to full mobility which, though advised as a possibility for which both of us earnestly hoped and eagerly worked, was never completely realised. But my wife never gave up trying, and it was thanks to her resolution—without which the best of medical skill would have been unavailing—that, strapped up with what was to my unprofessional eye a heavy and burdensome pair of callipers, she took once more a few hesitant steps.

The silver lining to this very dark cloud was the immense kindness of my Australian comrades, the Sydneysiders in particular. The leading bands in the city took turns on a Sunday morning to visit the Prince Alfred Hospital. The women folk, both officers and soldiers, showed their concern for her as if she had been a sister. When I left for the High Council on Monday, September 9th, Colonel Olive Allitt, then our Women's Social Secretary, arranged for her transfer to our own 'Bethesda' hospital. Fortified by this union of skill and care our joint hopes were high when we finally left Australia on the *Oriana* on Saturday, October 26th, 1963. Daily we found a secluded part of the deck where walking could be practised. Even after we had reached International Headquarters this exercise was continued in the dinner hour up and down the narrow carpeted corridor which runs alongside the offices of the General and his wife. It would have been unkind to have had her go with me to Asia and Africa, but her utter determination—coupled with the daily consideration of Salvationists and friends in general— upheld her in campaigns which we conducted together in Europe and North America as well as in this country. That she continued to play even a limited part in public life until her promotion to Glory on December 12th, 1967, was a triumph of the spirit over the weakness of the flesh.

One of the most moving tributes to reach me was from a former non-Salvationist pupil of her teaching days at the John Howard (Clapton) Secondary School.

She was *truly* beautiful, very popular, infinitely patient, always friendly. We flocked to her classes. An excellent teacher, she made science exciting, yet simple and easy to understand, showing us how to work little miracles! She opened my mind to the vast universe and, to this day, I see a 'wide, beautiful, wonderful world'.

Her simplicity always came through . . . The whole school showed considerable excitement over her marriage . . . I met her only once since then, but all my life she made me think of Cowper's line: 'Calm and serene my frame'.

These personal references can end on a happier note for on December 31st, 1970, I was married to Commissioner Olive Gatrall who, prior to her retirement earlier in the year, had been Vice-Principal for nine years, and Principal for six years, of the International College for Officers in South London. Our joint retirement is being turned to good account insofar as we continue to do of our own free will what long since we pledged ourselves to do.

To return to my departure from Sydney, there was one final surprise. As the liner moved out from the Cove we heard an Army band, but knew not which it was nor whence the music came. But as we leaned over the side we saw that the Petersham band was following us on a tug. Our cup of Australian kindness was being pressed down, shaken together and running over. For six years we had lived in the Sydney suburb of Hurstville and, when we were leaving, the Mayor spoke of the gratification felt by his Council and himself that an Australian had been chosen as the next international leader of The Salvation Army! Ill at ease as one is during any form of eulogy, I took that as one of the neatest—even if wholly unintentional—compliments ever paid by an Aussie to a Pommie.

8

Whether of These Thou Hast Chosen

THE HIGH COUNCIL is the world body of Salvation Army leaders legally summoned—as necessity may arise—to elect a new international leader. Each of my immediate predecessors has written about the High Council—General Orsborn in *The House of my Pilgrimage* concerning the election of General Carpenter in 1939 and his own in 1946; General Kitching in *A Goodly Heritage* of his election in 1954. My own knowledge is limited to the High Councils of 1954 and 1963—plus an entirely unofficial watching brief in 1969 and again in 1974. However, these experiences have provided some insights into both the certainties and the uncertainties of such occasions. Two can be mentioned.

One certainty is that there is no certainty. However assured his (or her) election may appear to be to a Council member who accepts nomination, no one has the result in his pocket. No conclusion is a foregone conclusion. This was demonstrated in the very first of these High Councils. A nominee may talk himself into—and out of—the office. This inexorable sifting is one of the several benefits of the days which High Council members spend together. Some who view these proceedings from afar may feel that the final decision should be reached with all possible speed. Otherwise are not members wasting their time? They are not! Always a proportion of those present have never attended a High Council before. Always a proportion have never met one another before. How can it be otherwise when most members have spent their active service in widely separated fields? And not a few have been so occupied with present duties as to have had little time to give to thoughts of a future General. In any case, the membership of the High Council cannot finally be determined until four months before the date of the retirement of the active General, though without doubt unofficial lists of members are compiled many times over. But as each member of a High Council has the right to propose one nominee for the ballot, it is as well that each should be as fully aware as possible of the abilities—and the limitations—of the officer whose name he may be putting forward. The fellowship of worship and the fellowship of discussion help to provide this essential knowledge.

The other certainty is that the election will be honourably conducted by honourable men and women. And further, that the requirement of a two-thirds majority ensures that the elected nominee represents a reasonable consensus of opinion. No one is elected on a marginal vote. No electoral jugglery can transform a minority vote into a decisive majority. Yet though this procedure is described—for want of a better term—as an election, nothing is less like an election in the ordinary usage of that word. There are no candidates though there are nominees. The atmosphere of the hustings is replaced by a spirit of prayer. Without doubt members hold their several views as to who should be elected, but there is no wheeling and dealing. I can testify that my vote has never been solicited, neither have I at any time solicited a vote for myself or anyone else, nor have I ever voted for myself. No man is fit to judge in his own cause.

> If self the wavering balance shake
> 'Tis rarely right adjusted.

While each High Council is free to formulate its own procedural arrangements, the guide lines laid down by previous High Councils are largely accepted for the proven wisdom which they embody. He has to be sure of his ground who would improve upon the ways of his elders. Nevertheless in

1963—and arising out of the thoughts expressed in the preceding paragraph—I had the temerity to move a resolution that 'no member of the High Council shall propose himself or herself as nominee for the office of General'. I had raised this point tentatively in 1954, but felt myself so inexperienced among my seniors that I withdrew the proposal without pressing it to a vote. This time I determined to stand my ground. The resolution was seconded, given what was officially described as 'very full and lengthy discussion' and was narrowly carried.

For my part, I felt such a self-denying ordinance to be essential if we were to remain faithful to our traditional discipline. Who should set an example to the officer corps of the Army in such matters if not its leaders? Our rule is to go where we are sent. Now and again an individual may refuse point blank but that is the rare exception. No officer touts for an appointment, though he is usually asked if he is willing to serve in a country other than his own. It would therefore be out of character to put one's own name forward for the heaviest responsibility of all. No officer writes out his own marching orders. (My Salvationist comrades will understand the phrase.) Nor can I write my own name in the 'marching orders' for the office of General. Others may do that; I must not.

When, with the other five nominees, I was called upon to address the High Council, I made three preliminary points.

The first is that I would apply to the office of a General a saying of John Quincy Adams concerning the Presidency of the United States—that it is an office neither to be solicited nor to be declined. I have not done the former, and happily the decision on the latter rests with the High Council.

The second is that in addressing you I am not running against any other nominee. This is not what in political circles might be called an election speech, designed to secure personal support. Rather do I regard it as part of our mutual thinking in order that we may come to a cor-

D

porate decision concerning the will of the Lord in this matter.

The third is that I draw a very clear distinction between the office of General and the person holding that office. The title of General does not confer infallibility. The utmost one can endeavour to do is to maintain one's own integrity.

What then followed was an endeavour to spell out three aims which would be followed in the event of being elected. The first would be:

To confirm the faith of the Army in its divine mission, by which I do not mean merely to praise our Founders or to pay lip service to their spirit. In one sense we have no need to praise them. The farther the years remove them from us, the greater do they grow . . .

Rather do we need to confirm our officers and soldiers in the faith that they have as significant a part to play in the redeeming purpose of God as their fathers before them . . . But though this deepening sense of our current mission can be born only of the Spirit, its practical out-working will demand the use of all our resources, mental and material, and of these we are not devoid . . .

In the second place, to confirm the faith of the Army in its place and function in the church universal. When our Founders parted company with that part of the church known as the Methodist New Connexion, I do not understand that they cut themselves off from the Body of Christ or the People of God. The oft-quoted words of General Bramwell Booth in chapter eight of 'Echoes and Memories' cannot be repeated too often. To assert our continuing place in the church universal is not to betray our Founders but to spell out what their action means for us today.

We must spell this out for our people—particularly for our young people—so that they may understand that they have no need to seek elsewhere for the essential grace which can be found within our own walls, nor can any churchly blessing make them more truly members of the heavenly kingdom than they are by faith in Jesus as Saviour and Lord.

And spell it out for our officers as well so that nowhere will any of them—woman or man, single or married—be received as any other than a minister of the gospel, 'as poor, yet making many rich; as having nothing, and yet possessing all things' . . .

In the third place, to confirm the faith of the Army in the integrity of its own government. This calls for informed leadership . . . especially when, as with our structure, a General is both the source of authority and the final court of appeal. This means that he must be free from the very appearance of partiality, and never allow any domestic conversation to interfere with, much less take the place of, the counsel of his appointed officers . . .

In this matter I have long reflected upon the very proper care we exercise in the spending of money. A voucher or bill submitted for payment will be scrutinised by the responsible departmental head, endorsed, and then passed for approval to the appropriate expenditure board whose members will examine the voucher or account after which two of them, one of whom is the chairman, approves the payment, and only then will a cheque—again requiring two signatures—be drawn. In short, no one can spend one penny of Salvation Army money at his own whim or pleasure. The same careful responsibility must be shown in all other forms of decision making—particularly those which involve the well-being of our officers and their families . . .

Before each of the nominees speaks, however, he is required to answer some twenty to thirty questions addressed to him by the High Council as a body. These vary from time to time but have mainly to do with matters of administration. Points of specific interest may also be covered as when, for example, in 1963 the need to prepare for the Centenary was urgent. This is an agreed way of conveying to the nominees what the Council feels should be the main concerns of the Movement. A nominee often shares such concerns, but the wise nominee will not deliver himself bound hand and foot to a particular solution. Not until he sits down in his office on the second floor at '101' and calls for the file will he know the truth, the whole truth, and nothing but the truth on some contentious point. He can say, of course, that he will give his earliest attention to the matter—and honestly abide by the spirit as well as the letter of his promise. But to announce a line of action in advance is to make an error of judgment. After all, no member of the High Council knows all the facts for none has ever sat in the General's chair.

There are also personal questions which can be addressed to a particular nominee. These may have to do with his past service, his present health or some future contingency. The sole personal question addressed to me had to do, very properly, with the health of my wife. (The President of the Council, Commissioner Norman Marshall, also made his own sympathetic private enquiry.) The health of the nominees had already been the subject of a general question and I could only repeat the substance of my earlier reply (given in the light of the best of my knowledge at the time) that my wife had 'recently suffered a post-vaccineal reaction which resulted in a temporary loss of the use of her legs. She is not yet fully recovered, but has now made sufficient progress to commence to walk with artificial aids . . . At no time has she been affected in spirit or in mind; rather is she fully determined to get better, and this is the end to which we both are working.'

Four ballots, covering a period of nearly three hours, had to be taken before the required two-thirds majority was reached, but just before five o'clock on Tuesday, October 1st, the election was over.

There are those who still make much of the supposed autocracy of the General of The Salvation Army. This is a tale which takes on a new lease of life whenever someone in the service of the news media is short of a leading question. One meets it from the supposedly informed as well as the plainly uninformed. If words were rightly handled by some whose profession it is to use them, this fable would long ago have died the death.

According to Webster, an autocrat is an undisputed sovereign who rules without any restriction—in other words, a despot. Of course, with the man who will admit no distinction between authority and autocracy, further discussion is vain. But even a cricket team has a captain. The cup final has a referee whose word is law. A band has to have a bandmaster; an orchestra a conductor. Someone has to see that the agreed rules are kept. The extreme left agrees with the extreme right that followers must toe the party line. Deviationism is the dirtiest of dirty words. There is the type who starts from the assumption that anyone in authority must be in the wrong. Vain to beseech him, in the bowels of Christ, whether he might not be mistaken. Experience has taught me that some of the most vehement of rebels are themselves the most implacable when 'drest in a little brief authority'.

But when the office of General is fairly examined, it is soon seen that he is, of all men, least fancy free. To begin with, he has not seized office by any ecclesiastical *coup d'état*. The odds are that he has not even sought office. I am no Pepys and my diaries contain little but the names of places visited, the mileage covered, the times of arrival and departure and a note of engagements fulfilled between these two points. But to make sure that my own mind was clear on essentials I did add six single-syllabled words against Thursday, September 19th, 1963: 'As Thou wilt, where Thou wilt'.

In this context wherein alone perfect freedom is to be found, a General can run his course within the guide lines of accepted principle and accredited counsel. These may not—indeed, they will not—provide him with a line of action which will please all parties at all times. Previous administrative experience will have taught him that there is a time to say yes, and a time to say no. Never is he more in need of this combination of discernment and resolution than as General. To try to resolve any difficulty merely by seeking the easy way out would be to do despite to his appointment and be the beginning of the end of his influence. The office of General is not an exercise in public relations. Some decisions may be comparatively easy to reach because the issues at stake are so well

defined. Yet those may be the very decisions whose implementation may be painful to others and embarrassing to
himself. Yet such consequences must be personally borne,
not in any bitterness of spirit and extravagance of language,
but with such quietude of heart and speech as Christian grace
may provide. 'I have never found it necessary to raise my
voice,' General Carpenter once said to me—a counsel never
forgotten even though not always practised.

Again, a General cannot, off his own bat, override existing
Salvation Army discipline. He could not, for example, annul
the regulation which requires every salvation soldier to be a
total abstainer. Nor can he disobey the regulations to which he
requires his people to conform. This was made clear more
than forty years ago when General E. J. Higgins was being
cross-examined by Mr. W. E. Tyldesley Jones before the
House of Commons Select Committee which was examining
The Salvation Army Bill, 1931. Discussing the framing and
operating of Salvation Army regulations Mr. Jones said: 'You
meant, did you not, that if a General framed regulations for
the good of the Army he, at all events, would not depart from
them himself?' 'Yes,' answered General Higgins, 'I am
certainly under the impression that a General should be
bound by those regulations.'

So un-autocratic (to coin a word) is the Army's mode of
government that there is a procedure to be followed—and
again this goes back more than forty years—should there arise
any 'difference, misunderstanding or grievance' between a
General and officers of specified rank and/or responsibility.
Now if a willingness on the part of a leader to be taken to task
by someone whom he himself has appointed, or who was
appointed by one or other of his predecessors, is described as
autocratic, then words have lost their meaning and rational
argument is no longer possible.

To drive a final nail into the coffin of this hoary invention,
let reference be made to the action of General Orsborn in
1947 in setting up the 'Advisory Council to the General'.
This idea had been mooted at the 1939 High Council, but
the outbreak of the Second World War had prevented any-

thing but a preliminary survey of Army opinion. This could not be other than incomplete, for by this time England was isolated from Europe and from much of Asia. However, the basic structure of the Advisory Council and the character of its work were formulated within less than twelve months of General Orsborn's accession to office—since when its procedures have been under constant review so that the Council may truly fulfil its original purpose.

Certain matters must be submitted to the Advisory Council; nominees for the office of General give this undertaking before going to the ballot. Any other matter may be considered at the wish of the General, but neither he nor the Chief of the Staff are members of the Advisory Council. The Council's own chairman forwards its recommendations to the General under confidential cover, though these need not be unanimous and provision is made for minority observations. The Council has its own secretary; keeps its own papers; can call for any document which might assist its deliberations and require the presence of any officer whose experience might be of service. As the Council's proceedings are private I cannot be more explicit, but possibly all but a dozen of the more than eight hundred recommendations placed before the General in the last quarter of a century have been accepted by him. In view of these facts perhaps we may now hope to hear no more of his supposedly despotic exercise of power.

The election over, my concern was to return to Sydney and then get back to London. The deadline was Saturday, November 23rd; it was now Tuesday, October 1st—and the homeward journey would have to be made by sea. I left Heathrow at 10 a.m. on Friday, October 4th and, with stops at Zurich, Cairo, Abadan, Bombay, Colombo, Kuala Lumpur, Singapore, Perth (Monday, October 7th at 4.15 a.m.), arrived in Sydney by 11 a.m. the same day. That was the measured speed of the piston engine age whether the plane was described as a 'Skymaster' or a 'Constellation'. Australian Salvationists, complete with band, were present at the Perth airport to greet me. They may not have been half-asleep—but I was!

The remaining rituals of packing and parting would never

have been completed without the loyal help of my comrade of many years, the Chief Secretary of the Eastern Territory, the then Colonel Henry Warren and the indefatigable Mrs. Warren, whose good works were never more greatly needed, nor more freely given, than during those final days. As Elizabeth, my wife and myself watched the Sydney Heads fading from view, we consoled ourselves with the motto of the School of the Air: 'Parted yet united'!

9

The Field is the World

WHEN ON MONDAY, November 25th, 1963, I entered for the first time the General's office on the second floor of the newly opened International Headquarters, I realised that I was entering into other men's labours—particularly those of my predecessor, General Wilfred Kitching. Her Majesty Queen Elizabeth the Queen Mother had formally opened the building on the previous November 13th, and ten days later the General retired from active service. It was as if he had gladly sung his *Nunc dimittis* now that the new headquarters had risen from the ashes of the old.

The original '101' was acquired by William Booth in 1881 and by the night of May 10th/11th, 1941, the International and Associated Headquarters covered the whole block from Lambeth Hill on the east to Benet's Hill on the west, with the administrative offices of the British Territory on the opposite side of the street. It was obvious from the beginning that to rebuild on a comparable scale would be a herculean effort but, though the various headquarters had to be scattered throughout the Greater London area, in faith the Army's registered address remained '101, Queen Victoria Street'.

In 1948 the City of London set up its own enquiry at the Guildhall to determine who should, or should not, be allowed to rebuild within the city boundaries. General Orsborn arranged that the Army should be legally represented but, even before we were called upon to speak, Sir Walter Monckton, counsel for the City, rose to say that it was the wish of the authorities that the Army should remain within 'the square mile'.

This was the first hurdle overcome, but planning difficulties seemed to be endless—one of several being the need to promote a special Act of Parliament to close the graveyard of the former church of St. Peter in Upper Thames Street, and arrange for the removal to Manor Park Cemetery of some eighty coffins of victims of the Great Fire of London in 1666. Any new building had to conform to the overall city plan, but finally it was agreed that the new headquarters should be sited so as to lie clear of the proposed St. Paul's Vista. The Army already held the freehold of nos. 101–107 and the City of London generously made over those of nos. 97 and 99. Meanwhile General Orsborn had retired so that the burden of the needful fund-raising fell upon his successor, but literally the whole Army world rallied to his support so that *The War Cry* could announce that the target for Britain would not be more than £200,000. As a point of interest, within three months of the destruction of the old property the St. Albans corps—to which I belonged from 1940 to 1953 and again from 1969 to date— had given £101 for the rebuilding of '101'. This was part of the inheritance upon which I was now privileged to enter.

Again, a new General inherits a tried and proven system of administration which has reached its present state of efficiency by the unforgiving processes of trial and error. Whether he wishes to or not, a General must accept this yoke. Small use murmuring that this serving of tables seems to have little to do with the work of evangelism. The sixth chapter of the Acts of the Apostles shows it to be an integral part of the work of the Holy Spirit. The church has to conduct her business as efficiently as does the world—else her first work, that of evangelism, will be the first to suffer. The International Headquarters of The Salvation Army has never been a place where its principal officers arrive late and go away early. A forty-hour week is not for them, for when they leave the office it is often to take up other essential work at home.

The Chief of the Staff is the administrative king-pin and,

quite early in the piece, Commissioner Erik Wickberg was generous enough to offer to accept another appointment but, swift as he was to make this suggestion, it was equally swiftly declined. His knowledge of European affairs was unrivalled and he had already profited from two-and-a-half years' experience as Chief. We worked happily together until in due course he himself was elected General, and no major decision was taken without prior consultation with him. The dawn of our Centenary Year saw International Headquarters in the fortunate position of having Commissioners Theo. Holbrook and Aage Rønager with Lieut.-Commissioner Edward Carey as the principal International Secretaries, each well versed in his field of responsibility; the informed and dependable Commissioner Arthur Pallant as Secretary to the Advisory Council to the General; Commissioner Frank Fairbank was a most experienced Chancellor; the gifted Commissioner Gilliard was Literary Secretary and Editor in Chief; that master of detail, Colonel J. H. Swinfen, was Secretary to the Chief of Staff, and Colonel Arnold Brown had just been brought over from Canada to give a new look to our public relations work. Lieut.-Commissioner Westcott and Commissioner Dorothy Muirhead were each bringing more than forty years' experience to the leadership of the Men's and Women's Social Services respectively, and I had asked Commissioner William F. Cooper to assume the command of the British Territory, with Lieut.-Commissioner Mingay continuing to have oversight of the six Scottish divisions. A captain would have had to be a dolt to fail with a team like that.

But a General inherits a world ministry as well. As the Army's international leader he is expected to visit each territory and command. Faced with this requirement I made a private rule that I would visit no territory twice until I had visited each territory once. My good intention could not be kept, for the European territories are accustomed to have the General or the Chief of the Staff lead their annual congresses on alternate years. However, every territory was visited though the commands of Italy and Burma were not. No excuse can be offered for the first omission but a visa was not forthcoming for Burma. Happily the position there is much easier and our Gideon's band in Rangoon is not so isolated as it once was.

Yet with all these world demands a General cannot afford to neglect Great Britain which, with over a thousand corps and goodwill centres, still remains the Army's largest single administrative unit. In terms of direct evangelism a British Commissioner will always have the heaviest burden to bear but he has also the support of a body of local officers and soldiery whose competence and dedication may be equalled, but cannot be out-rivalled, anywhere in the Army world. It may be thought that I am biased in favour of the land of the Army's birth, but as with Salvation Army bands, I have no favourites for each is my favourite.

Within twenty-four hours of taking office the news media expect a General to outline his future aims and specifically his new plans. In one sense this is a question he cannot answer. Our basic aim—the proclamation of the saving power of the gospel—remains the same from General to General. We know where our mission lies. We have no desire to extend our borders at the expense of any other church. Our constituency is made up of the vast number of otherwise decent men and women who regrettably sit loosely to the claims of the Christian faith. Of course there are the deliberate rogues, the crooks and the pimps, but many of the socially inadequate—to use the euphemism of our time—are more to be pitied than blamed. Yet we do not serve their true interests by condoning their sad ways in the name of the divine charity which would redeem them from their evil power. Whatever our personal reading of the state of the western world the communication of the gospel remains both our chief duty and our leading problem, and early in my term of office the Joystrings made a significant breakthrough.

Captain Joy Webb was then an officer on the International Training College who had already begun to experiment with washboards and tea chest basses in open-air work at the seaside and industrial centres. In response to a question at an early press conference as to what new methods we might follow, I had answered that it might be a worthwhile idea to try to communicate with the young folk found in coffee bars and amusement arcades by means of guitar groups or similar informal parties.

'You mean,' said my interlocutor, 'that you want to be "with it"?'

'If you put it like that,' I answered.

He did not know, nor did I, that the Joystrings already existed in embryo. But no one could have anticipated the storm that broke over my head—but most woundingly over the eager and defenceless heads of the young officers who were concerned only to do service for the Kingdom. I was old enough and tough enough to endure the near-abuse of those who declared that the Army uniform was being befouled when the Joystrings played for three consecutive nights at 'The Blue Angel'. In reality all they were doing was to sing their original gospel songs, interspersed with their own personal testimony, while some of their comrades at the training college had set their alarm clocks for 2 a.m. so that they could support them in prayer. Some church leaders who professed an interest in evangelism shook their heads gravely. Pejorative paragraphs appeared in some religious weeklies. In vain I searched my files for reports of parallel admonitions addressed to the present Bishop of Stepney when he founded the Huddleston jazz band in Sophiatown twenty years earlier. Nor were we spared chastisement at the hands of certain of our own elder brethren, though some of these were so distant from London as to depend on third-hand information. When I answered in a befitting spirit of meekness there were those who replied to assure me that I was either deliberately blind or being deliberately gulled. But they were forgetting their own history—and no movement can afford to do that. Part of our own incomparable story is that General Bramwell Booth once appeared as twelfth on the programme in a Plymouth music hall, the orchestra cueing him on stage with 'For he's a jolly good fellow', and the audience giving him a standing ovation as he left. Between these two he preached the gospel—as did the Joystrings.

However, when to the Baptist Hymnal has now been added 'Praise for Today', to the English Hymnal 'English Praise', to Ancient and Modern 'One hundred hymns for today', and to the publications of the Church of Scotland 'Songs for the Seventies', the Joystrings may well feel that their modest 'It's an open secret' has borne an abundant harvest. But they could deem themselves both acceptable and accepted when invited to play on behalf of Christian Aid on the steps of St. Paul's Cathedral where a press photographer caught Dean Matthews smiling his approval. Wisdom was even more justified of her children when, at a Sunday afternoon rally in a Tokyo park at which I was present, a uniformed rhythm group from the corps at Hiroshima played and sang.

A ball by ball account of a General's travels could easily become wearisome to the reader. In essentials one modern airport is very like another. Each has its exits and its entrances; each its lounges where impatient travellers await the call for their departure door; each its coffee bars and duty free counters though not—up to 1969 at any rate—its established frisking points. Not until after retirement did I discover that an Army badge could ring the metal detector device, whereupon one was promptly given the full treatment. The principal virtue of air travel is that it offers the shortest distance in the quickest time between any two given points on the map.

It is with some wry amusement that in recent days I have read the solemn warnings addressed to the business men of this world not to take any personal decisions until their physical mechanisms have had opportunity to adjust themselves to the time changes which long distance travel involves. It can only be wished that any thus afflicted had left Heathrow with me at fifteen hours on a chilly January afternoon and alighted at Bombay at six-thirty the following morning—to feel the heat of the day already rising in waves from the runway; at ten-thirty to address a private conference, at eighteen hours a public rally, with the formal opening of a new Salvation Army property thrown in for good measure in the afternoon. Lest anyone thinks that this example is specially picked out of the hat, try leaving Gatwick for Brazil at twenty-one hours, changing at Rio de Janeiro for the last two hundred and fifty miles from a VC 10 to a Fokker, arriving at São Paulo at ten o'clock (local time), with a reception laid on at the airport, a press conference to follow, a courtesy call on the state governor at seventeen hours and an address to the English-speaking community at eighteen-thirty hours.

Some of these courtesy calls had a quality all of their own. One would arrive at the appointed hour, be cordially welcomed, escorted to a waiting room on the ground floor and invited to take coffee. After a while the excellence of the coffee could not wholly quell the rising unease at the delay but, before this became unbearable, another functionary would appear with an invitation to come up higher. Tunics were straightened, throats cleared, this was the moment—but on the next floor another door would open, another arm chair wait invitingly and another coffee be suggested. It would be churlish to decline such an offer from an attendant so eager to demonstrate the merits of his brew, so another coffee—making, serving and drinking— would occupy another fifteen minutes. It seemed that the ritual could be repeated as frequently as might be necessary, but I sought comfort in George Herbert's observation: 'God taketh a text, and preacheth patience.'

Nothing must surprise a General on his travels. He can be received with royal informality as at Soestdijk where Queen Juliana poured coffee as an easy flowing conversation revealed her genuine interest in the welfare of her people. Or with the ceremonial formality of the Emperor Hirohito where, supported by the gentle Commissioner Koshi Hasegawa on the right hand and the sturdy Colonel Yasowo Segawa on the left, I spoke as etiquette required through an interpreter through whom the Emperor also replied, though it was no secret that royalty understood English.

Nor must he display the least embarrassment when a friendly host, meeting him at the door and leading him with all due courtesy through the hallway, suggests a sherry—until an alert A.D.C., more versed in the ways of this world, moves up on His Excellency's offside, whereupon the proposal is amended to: 'Perhaps a coffee, then.' Nor when, calling upon the Senior Chief of the Ba-Venda, he is serenaded by several hundred musicians producing their own unique brand of harmony as each performer blows the one fixed note which his pipe can

produce, somewhat after the manner of our handbell ringers—
but with much more cacophonous results. Nor when, moving
in procession through a Gujerati village in order to declare
well and truly laid the foundation stone of a new Army hall,
he finds high and lifted up and moving in step with him on the
one side an ancient picture of William Booth and, on the other,
a companion picture of the Vicar of Christ.

Nor when, landing on Antigua in the Leeward Islands, he
discovers himself to be at the head of a cavalcade of some thirty
cars, all provided by the local trade unions, and is taken by a
circuitous route into St. John's in order that the widest possible
announcement may be made by loud hailer of his arrival. Nor
when, seated in his allotted chair on the platform at Moratuwa
listening to words of welcome, there is a sudden explosion
above his head and, in the twinkling of an eye, he is generously
showered with confetti. It was only much later that I learnt
that this was to be accepted as a mark of singular regard. At the
time there was nothing I could do but to thank the congregation for their unique welcome and disappear from sight to
brush the confetti out of my ears. Salvationists will be relieved
to know that the event did not detract from the spirit of the
meeting, but I thought this cautionary word should appear as
a warning to any future visitors.

Nor can a General hesitate to answer any call, from whatever
quarter it may come, to which it is physically possible for him
to respond. One of the first lessons taught to Cadets in training
is that they are to be 'servants of all'—not just of those whose
names appear on a Salvation Army roll. So when the telephone
rang one Sunday midday to ask me to conduct the funeral of
Lord Morrison of Lambeth on Thursday, March 11th, 1965,
the answer was an immediate yes. Thus in the setting of a
Salvation Army funeral which, by the absence of all conventional signs of mourning, testifies to the truth that though
things seen are temporal, the things which are not seen are
eternal, and in the presence of a congregation which ranged
from peers of the realm to the pearly king and queen of Lambeth, filling the chapel and overflowing on to the lawns outside,
the words were heard which commit the souls of the departed

to 'the certainty of the resurrection and the eternal wisdom and mercy of God.'

Sometimes a call will come from a priest who feels that the witness of the Army will further the effectiveness of his own ministry, as when the Rev. Nicholas Stacey asked that we conduct a Sunday evening meeting in the Woolwich Parish Church. I do not think that Mr. Stacey mistrusted what a Salvationist might say in his pulpit, but he gave me my topic and my text. No matter! What counts is not so much the starting point as the way that is taken and the goal that is reached. So we began in true Salvation Army fashion with an open-air meeting, followed by a march in which the Army flags flanked the processional cross and the open Bible was borne by the session clerk of the neighbouring Presbyterian church. The church was full; the band played; the choir joined with the songsters for the evening, and man's common salvation was proclaimed from the appointed text.

Sometimes a call will come which may have a few gins and snares concealed. In the summer of 1969 I was invited to share in a televised religious programme. I had a pricking of my thumbs that all might not be well and so was not wholly surprised when I found my interrogators armed with quotations from Jack London and Beatrice Webb with which—fortunately —I was also familiar. The former had dilated at some length on the treatment he received on a Sunday morning in 1902 when, posing as one of seven hundred down and outs, he attended the free breakfast given in our Blackfriars shelter. Beatrice Webb visited the Hadleigh Land Colony for a week-end in 1908 and, though questioning what she called 'the religious pressure' exercised in the Sunday evening meeting, praised in warmest terms the 'courtesy' and 'open-mindedness' of the staff. Perhaps the programme planners had written me off as a rabbit. If so, they met a rabbit in a rage for I was not to be put down with selective quotations of ancient vintage. 'If you use either of these (I warned them before the cameras started rolling) as a stick wherewith to beat the Army, I shall interrupt to say that you had to go back sixty years to find your weapon.' Jack London and Beatrice Webb were not so much as mentioned, though the interviewer tried to recover lost ground by opening the discussion on the Christian faith by asking me: 'You surely don't believe all that codswallop?' Remembering how Partridge defines the word, the remark deserved to be ignored.

Sometimes a call will come asking for an explanation of one of our Salvation Army principles—for example, the place of women in our Movement. By invitation I was able, on two separate occasions, to speak about our practice to the Roman Catholic St. Joan's International Alliance and the Anglican Society for the Ministry of Women in the Church. Apart from a lively awareness of my own limitations I have never been unwilling to stand in any setting in my uniform to give a reason for the hope that is in me. The compulsion to do so transcends any ecclesiastical differences. The Salvationist refuses to share in any sectarian quarrels. As George Whitfield told the Seceders in Dunfermline: 'If the Pope himself would lend me his pulpit I would gladly proclaim the righteousness of Jesus Christ therein.'

10

High and Low Estate

IT MUST NOW be clear that one of the uncovenanted enrich-
ments of a Salvation Army officer's life is the wide range
of men and women whom he meets in the course of duty,
though it might not have been surprising had I suffered
from a lifelong fixation concerning those of high estate.
Psychiatrists specializing in child studies may deduce what
they wish to deduce from the fact that, as a small boy, I was
barred from one of the Founder's meetings. It happened on
this wise. In the lobbies and access ways of such halls as
were hired for his public gatherings during the opening
decade of the present century would appear a notice in large
red letters:

> CHILDREN UNDER FIVE (WITH
> OR WITHOUT THEIR PARENTS)
> ARE NOT ADMITTED.

I must have passed my fourth birthday and been capable
(under due constraint) of behaving myself, but no Garden of
Eden was more effectively guarded by implacable cherubim than
the entrances and exits of that west-country theatre. The
ancient story speaks of one flaming sword which turned
every way. In this twentieth-century story there was a sword
at every passage way. My young mother, in her officer's
uniform and not unattractive in her early thirties, hurried

from door to door, but at each the forbidding sign in letters of fire rose before us. She did not hear, nor did I see, William Booth, on that Sunday afternoon.

What irreparable harm was done to my childish psyche who can tell? This may be—or, on the other hand, it may not be—the reason why I took the trouble to hear, but never dared approach, some of the men of high estate in the inter-war period—W. B. Selbie, then Principal of Mansfield College, who came to a Glasgow pulpit for an August season; J. E. Rattenbury who visited the red-brick church which used to stand almost opposite what was the Central Station in Black-pool; F. B. Meyer—half-sitting, half-resting—on a tallish stool as he occupied a Baptist pulpit in Chatham; W. R. Maltby in a South London mission hall; A. J. Gossip in a Rothesay church; Dinsdale Young in Wesley's Chapel; J. D. Jones in his prime at Richmond Hill—the cathedral of Congre-gationalism as it used to be called. The fact that I was stationed in Bournemouth for three years gave me an opportunity of inviting him to the Army. Somewhat daringly for a junior officer, I had enquired whether the Chief of the Staff, the then Commissioner E. J. Higgins, could visit our corps at Winton and, drawing yet another bow at a venture, invited Dr. Jones to preside at the Sunday afternoon rally. In those days J. D. conducted as much of his correspondence as he could on postcards. The postage was then a half-penny, and in due course I received a hand-written postcard. This was J.D.'s first visit to the Army, and for that occasion I think we provided him with a congregation which may even have been larger than those which he drew Sunday by Sunday at Richmond Hill.

About this time I was fortunate enough to spend ten days of my annual furlough at a summer school which was run each year by the Society of Friends at Selly Oak. As a recently married Army officer I could not have paid even the modest fee required, but somehow screwed up my courage to enquire whether there were any bursaries! Whether there were or not, the organisers had compassion on me, and so my world was widened as I listened to, and shared in subsequent discussions with, Arthur Eddington (not yet knighted), the Plumian Professor of Astronomy, who two years earlier had unveiled the mind of Einstein to the English-speaking world in his 'Mathematical Theory of Relativity'; Alison Peers, an established authority on Spanish mysticism; H. G. Wood—in whose honour there is now a chair of theology at the University of Birmingham; and Rendel Harris, who was related by marriage to our own Major Margaret Balkwill of the Women's Social Services, and who testified that 'some of his greatest illuminations had come to him in an Army barracks amid the clashing of tambourines.'

It was said that he had added an extra petition to the Lord's prayer: 'Give us day by day our daily discovery.' I was granted a few at Woodbrooke—one of which was the confirmation of my growing understanding that there need be no conflict between the enquiring mind and the devout heart. To question is not to doubt. To examine a truth simply means that we want to know more about it. There was no denying the immense erudition of the beloved doctor, but he also spoke to God as a man communeth with his friend—freely but never familiarly for true friendship is never unmannerly. Our own John Murfitt enjoyed the same respectful but happy liberty.

On second thoughts, the phrase in the previous paragraph about 'sharing in discussions with' is to look back through rose-coloured glasses. What really happened was that my silent wonder grew that so few heads could carry all they knew.

The mid-thirties in London provided me with an enriching fellowship with Canon W. E. S. Holland, then Vicar of the Guild Church of St. Mary Woolnoth. He was running at the time a well-attended series of weekly lunch-hour services in which I was asked to share and, on a subsequent occasion, to bring along a Salvation Army team of witness. The Vicar spared no effort to maintain the standard of these twenty-five minute gatherings, but I recall my private surprise when the name of D. S. Cairns, then Principal of the United Free Church (now Christ's) College, Aberdeen, was announced. Later I enquired whether Dr. Cairns had come all that way

for this one short service. He had. I went away thoughtful.
Here was someone who felt it worthwhile to travel more
than a thousand miles to commend—be it never so briefly—
the Christian gospel.

But St. Mary Woolnoth knew its largest congregation when
Dick Sheppard took the pulpit. Not only was every pew
almost too crowded for comfort but city gents lined the walls
and filled the porch. The speaker began by saying that, having
in mind the importance of any city gathering, he had prepared
with every care but, on the way in, had mislaid his notes.
Dick Sheppard expressed the hope that he had not left them
in the taxi which had brought him to the church; the unfortunate driver might find them too dry for his digestion. But
the subsequent address was anything but dry.

This link with St. Mary Woolnoth brought me in touch
with Lord (then Dr.) Soper, for speakers at the three-hour
service on Good Friday circulated between Kingsway Hall,
St. Mary Woolnoth and one other city church. And somehow,
during the blitz, I found myself at the Westminster Central
Hall where Dr. Sangster was determinedly maintaining his
ministry despite the terror by night. His Sunday evening
meetings at this time were happy and informal, intended
to sustain the morale of the substantial congregation which
still gathered despite wartime hazards. This suited me, for I
never pretended to be other than I was—a Salvation Army
officer whose only virtue was a desire to make the Christian
message clear and plain. The choir was to sing at the close of
the address—and there took place as neat and unobtrusive a
piece of adaptation as I had seen. Whatever anthem may
have been planned, within sixty seconds the choir was singing
from the section of the Methodist Hymn Book entitled 'The
gospel call' or, in our Salvation Army song book, 'The news
of salvation'. I went away with a possible word stored up for
our own songster brigades.

Australia brought further enrichment. Even the asperities
of the political life of the Commonwealth might have been
softened had not Viscount Dunrossil passed away so untimely
after less than two years as Governor-General. The Aussies

were eager to know how, as W. S. Morrison, he had fared as Speaker of the British House of Commons from 1951 to 1959. They were aware that their own assembly could be a shade tumultuous at times. By way of answer he told of the Irish farmer with seven adult sons. 'Those are fine boys of yours,' said a visitor. 'How do you get on with them?' 'Very well indeed,' was the answer. 'I've never had to lift a hand to any one of them—except in self-defence!' As a parable of leadership the story was not without point.

The Rt. Hon. J. G. Diefenbaker also made no small impression—on me, at any rate—when he visited Australia during his term as Prime Minister of the Dominion of Canada. The government of New South Wales gave a reception for him in the city of Sydney and, from my seat below the salt, I could see Mr. Diefenbaker with the Premier, the Hon. J. J. Cahill, on the one side and His Eminence, Cardinal Gilroy, on the other. As is usual on these occasions, the wining is on the house and there are always those who take advantage of this fact. Through the haze of cigar smoke which hung over the top table I noted Mr. Diefenbaker's glass—of milk!

Membership of the Australian Council of Churches brought me in touch with the religious leaders of the six states—particularly those of New South Wales and Queensland. After eleven years in western China the Most Rev. H. W. K. Mowll reigned in Sydney as Archbishop and was a venerable figure when we paid our initial respects to him in 1957. He was succeeded in 1959 by the Rt. Rev. H. R. Gough, formerly Suffragan Bishop of Barking, during whose term as Primate the autonomy of the Anglican Communion in Australia was constitutionally recognised. This had long been accepted *de facto*, but with the approval of the twenty-five diocesan synods, and the enactment of the appropriate legal instruments by the six state parliaments, the Anglican church in the Commonwealth formally became mistress in her own house. On Tuesday, May 8th, 1962, in the Chapter House in Sydney and in the presence of the Governor General, representatives from the non-Anglican churches were invited to mark this new development. The Primate mercifully delivered the company from an undesired spate of repetitive speeches by asking the guests to express their good wishes in a letter which we each presented to him in turn before the Synod. Other masters of assemblies, please copy where possible.

We had many good friends among the clergy and ministers, among whom I came to hold in respect Bishop Moyes of Armidale and the then Bishop Coadjutor in Sydney, Clive Kerle. Mrs. Moyes once spoke to my wife about her private pleasure whenever she entered the Army hall in Armidale, at that time a very unpretentious wooden structure. 'I like coming here. I feel that this place has been prayed in,' were her words. Another genuine wellwisher was the Rev. Bernard Judd, the evangelical secretary of the New South Wales Council of Churches. When it seemed as if the municipality of Randwick would deny the Army the right to purchase any land in that suburb on which to build a hall, and we staged a public protest alongside the site we wished to buy, Mr. Judd shared our demonstration with us of his own accord.

Nor can anyone interested in the Christian faith be long in Sydney without hearing the name of the Rev. Alan Walker of the Methodist Central Mission. He was speaking like a Salvationist when recently he declared that, had he a dictator's power, he would direct the church to redeem Sunday night for mission. 'The church in the theatre, the church in the hall, the church in the open air would become commonplace . . . The organ would go. The organ tube is not the only pipe through which the Holy Spirit is heard . . . I would oblige every church to speak and plan for the nurture of Christians in the morning and go on mission in the evening.' Mr. Walker should know. In my years in Sydney he frequently enlisted the support of one or other of our several fine city bands for his Sunday afternoon people's rallies.

After returning to England in 1963 I found that unwittingly I gave Archbishop Lord Fisher of Lambeth—by this time retired to the Trent Rectory at Sherborne—cause to take me to task.

The Report of the Archbishops' Commission on 'Women in Holy Orders', presided over by the then Bishop of Chester,

Dr. Gerald Ellison, was published towards the end of 1966. *The Times* summed up the report in a three column headline: 'Admitting women into ministry would be divisive'. Perhaps the Commission had felt unable to do more than advance certain recommendations on the status and function of deaconesses because its terms of reference were 'to make a thorough examination of the various reasons for withholding the ordained and representative priesthood from women'. It may not be unfair to say that positive proposals were hardly to be expected from so negative a directive, but there were other 'asides' in the report which I felt could not go by default. So my letter to *The Times* for December 22nd read:

> Arising out of the publication of 'Women and Holy Orders', it is not my desire to suggest what any other church should do, but rather to speak from experience so far as The Salvation Army is concerned.
>
> We have probably a greater proportion of women to men serving in the pastoral office, as might be expected when appointments are made to men and women alike on the sole basis of character and competence.
>
> Certain observations attached to the report seem to fear that 'a bisexual priesthood' could exacerbate personal jealousies within the ministry itself and, as between pastor and people, 'spiritual intimacy' could 'spill over into incipient love relationships'.
>
> Our experience is the contrary. For men and women freely to associate in the highest of divine offices leads to a healthier respect the one for the other and a happier use of their complementary gifts. This is also reflected in their relationships with those for whom they have spiritual responsibility in a more wholesome attitude to the problems of life—including the man/woman relationship itself.
>
> Not the sex—but a sense of vocation, personal godliness and intellectual capacity are the necessary qualifications for a minister of religion.

Lord Fisher took me up on a point which was not—or so

I thought—at issue. To him the phrase 'not my desire to suggest what any other church should do' seemed 'to imply that The Salvation Army is itself a church'. His impression was the opposite.

In reply I covered familiar ground:

... So far as our position is concerned, over many years now The Salvation Army has been a 'church' in the accepted understanding of the word. As such we were represented at the 1937 conferences on 'Life and Work' at Oxford and 'Faith and Order' in Edinburgh. In 1948 we became a constituent member of the World Council of Churches . . .

We have our articles of faith which appear as an end paper in our song books, and a regular 'ministry' of men and women officers commissioned (i.e. 'ordained') . . . to conduct public worship, to offer the means of grace, to marry and to bury, to care for our soldiers (i.e. our committed membership) and, without interfering with the church affiliation of any, to seek to bring into the Kingdom those who are outside the pale of organised religion . . .

In answer Lord Fisher was good enough to provide a definition of the word 'church'—a definition which (he said) had won approval from 'distinguished persons in five or six different churches' whom he had consulted. This read:

The universal church of Christ, holy catholic and apostolic, is the visible society of the people of Christ, militant here on earth. Entry into this church is by the sacrament of baptism by water in the name of the Father, and of the Son, and of the Holy Ghost.

The Archbishop continued:

Every word of this definition has been carefully weighed. It rests entirely on the evidence provided in the New Testament. It is therefore in the full sense of the word *basic* [Lord Fisher's italics] for all doctrine about the church.

From it follows the right of the particular churches to hold their place in the universal church, and the call to all particular churches to find their way into full communion with one another in the sacrament of holy communion.

To this I had to reply or forever hold my peace, so I briefly reiterated our non-sacramental position, emphasising our belief that 'those who make a profession of faith in Christ as Saviour, and whose subsequent conformity to the Christian way of life supports that profession, are undeniably members of the church universal.' A further paragraph read:

In one sense we would not contend for the title of 'church' as if this conferred some kind of ecclesiastical status additional to that which we now possess. But I have to add that we are not an 'Order' within any existing church, much less a social agency. If I am asked for a definition which would include The Salvation Army, I give that of Bishop Stephen Neill: 'The church is that company of people who acknowledge Jesus as God and Saviour, and in whose midst the Holy Spirit is manifest.'

Lord Fisher pronounced Bishop Neill's definition as inadequate and offered further guidance on the difference between the church militant and the church invisible—i.e. the mystical body of Christ. I confess that this time I wrote more frankly:

If the ruling is that none but baptised persons can belong to the church here on earth, then I can only ask leave to dissent and to let the matter rest. For by all the tenor of the New Testament I cannot bring myself to agree that a man who has made a profession of faith in Jesus, and whose life by the aid of the Holy Spirit agrees with that profession, is outside the church of which that same Jesus is Lord. If the church visible—in the sense in which your Lordship uses the term—rejects us, then we can but commit ourselves to the truth that 'the Lord knoweth them that are His'.

The word 'rejects' was itself rejected. This (said the Arch-bishop) was 'a sign of remaining bitterness'. For one whose desire to share in the Christian witness of the historic churches, while yet maintaining the Army's identity, had provoked the criticism of some of his own comrades, this was a hard saying. However, I offered to substitute the milder word 'excludes', and Lord Fisher concluded the exchange by saying that 'it was the privilege of godly people to differ in amity.' If any reader wonders where the Army now stands, we remain a member of the World Council of Churches.

Very soon afterwards I was smitten on the other cheek for taking part with the Methodist and Roman Catholic churches in a Good Friday procession of witness in central London. The Rev. Dr. D. Martyn Lloyd-Jones, whose ministry at Westminster Chapel has been a cause of praise to God by many hearts, saw this—and similar happenings—as a sign of 'a Romeward tendency' on our part.

I was saddened by this judgment, for I had already tried to explain that our over-riding principle was our willingness to testify to the saving power of the gospel in any setting. This we had done, and would continue to do, in the street, in the public house, in prison, in hospital, in church—in short, anywhere at any time. Indeed, some bright spirit once asked whether our International Staff Band could not take part in the evening festival at the Royal Albert Hall which concluded the annual band contest. To this the answer was yes—so long as the band was allowed to make an act of Christian witness—that is to say, between their entry and departure to play a selection (or selections) of Salvation Army music, to offer prayer, to read a scripture portion and to sing a Salvation Army song. These were the basics of our own festivals of praise, and we were ready to do the same in any company anywhere else. It must be understood by our well-wishers and critics alike that we will continue to use to the full all the gifts which God has been pleased to grant us in pursuance of our Christian mission, but we will not employ the least of those gifts to further any other cause.

But to return to this particular march of witness, the following sentences from the correspondence restated our position:

> ... When we share (in united church rallies) we go to witness to our faith. Our flag—with its references to the Cross and Pentecost, 'Blood and Fire'—heads the march. Our people are in full uniform—and that speaks for itself ... Just as we work in countries which are almost wholly Roman Catholic—e.g. Mexico, Italy, Argentine, Chile, Brazil and so on—and there testify to the scriptural truth of salvation in the name of Jesus alone, so our participation in these united acts of witness is not a salute to any church, but a testimony to the saving power of Christ ...

Unhappily I laboured in vain. This was a sad breach in a **fellowship of the years—for it was Catherine Booth who** had advised the youthful Campbell Morgan not to become a Salvation Army officer but to enter the ministry, a fact which he himself never failed to acknowledge. Surely at this time of day no section of the church at large deems itself to possess a monopoly of saving truth. In a remote Swiss valley I once saw an hotel bearing the inscription: '*L'auberge au milieu du monde*'. May God save us all from the religious equivalent of such egoism.

There is, however, a brighter side to the coin. Recently I spent a weekend at one of our corps in central Lancashire. On the Monday evening an Army youth rally was held in the Methodist Central Hall at which one of the senior Roman Catholic priests in the town was present on the platform. He took no part save to admire the dexterity of the timbrellists and the skill of the young musicians. I had also been asked to present a new flag to three of the youth sections present and this I did, explaining—as is our custom—the meaning of the colours of the flag and drawing attention to the simple but significant Cross which surmounted each standard. Thus whenever we gathered with the flag for a religious service in the open air, it was in the shadow of the Cross. Wherever we marched it was with 'the Cross of Jesus going on before'.

I had been invited to remain for the Tuesday morning in order to speak to the clergy and ministers of the district about the work of the Army, with particular reference to the sacraments. I was encouraged to know that the corps officer was president of this group for the current year, but slightly apprehensive to be told that we were to meet in the presbytery. I feared that an ageing lion was to be thrown into a den of Daniels. In the discussion period my friend of the previous evening rose to his feet. 'My question,' he began, 'has little to do with what we have been talking about but, General, I was very moved last night by the presentation of your three standards to those young people. Would you please repeat what you said to the congregation for the benefit of my colleagues and myself?' So before this mixed group of Anglican, Roman Catholic and Free Church clergy and ministers, I once again explained the meaning of 'the yellow, the red and the blue'. Here was symbolised the Christian faith of those who followed the flag by virtue of the gift of the Spirit and in the power of the Blood. As Cardinal Manning once wrote to William Booth: 'Every living soul costs the most precious Blood,' and it is by the Blood of Jesus that believers in Christ are made one. Here, and not in any administrative readjustments, lies the true ecumenicity.

II

Faithful Brethren

'OUR PEOPLE WILL not process,' said a Free Church minister to me when, as a corps officer, I was trying to arrange a corporate act of Christian witness in the town where I was stationed. Once more I counted my blessings. My people would— and still will. There is a continuing necessity for a Christian presence in our streets when and where people are on the streets. Changes in shopping hours may have emptied the main thoroughfares of our provincial towns on a Saturday evening. The ubiquitous internal combustion engine now transports city dwellers in their thousands into the countryside during the summer, and the equally omnipresent television set helps to keep them indoors during the winter. Nevertheless Salvationists are still eager to maintain an effective public Christian witness.

Of course, I have read paragraphs disparaging the Army band 'blowing their heads off down some back street'— though I myself have not witnessed such a scene for many years. Point me out an Army bandsman who, in this year of musical grace, 'blows his head off'. As for 'down some back street', back streets are not unpopulated. Flesh and blood men and women still live there, and that is why the Army goes there. A casual observer may have noticed a group of uniformed bandsmen in a Scottish town disappearing into some close. There is method in their seeming madness. Within is what is often known as the back green and, rising high on

three sides, are the kitchen windows of the tenements whose
sitting rooms face the roadway in front. Public address equipment is hardly required. For better, for worse, both song and
speech are clearly audible in that confined setting. In such
a situation I always felt the need to weigh my words; someone
would be sure to be listening.

A rough survey of those back streets and closes might reveal
that a friendly and informal religious service is just what
those people need—and some may even want, for few are
regular attenders at any recognised place of worship. No
neighbourhood is without its lonely souls—as the 'meals on
wheels' service can testify. None is without families in sorrow.
None without its quota of lads and girls whose free-wheeling
ways have brought them to near disaster. Our Lord never said
that such would come flocking to our ecclesiastical doors. It
is we whom He calls to go to them. Let no one excuse himself
this inescapable Christian duty because a single broadcast
can provide an evangelist with a larger congregation than a
dozen meetings. The media may increase the number of
our hearers but we stand farther away from them. Political
parties know that no matter how high a rating their nation-
wide telecasts may secure, it is the door-to-door canvasser who
secures the promise of the vote. We can be duly grateful for
the opportunities provided by the media, but a person-to-
person confrontation is necessary to reap the full harvest.

Having marched the streets from being a young people's
bandmember, it is only natural that the sight and sound of an
Army march still—in Booth-Tucker's words—'make my pulse
fly'. And by this I do not mean only the set pieces such as the
Annual Congress march up to the Wellington town hall in
New Zealand, or that of Salvationists in Rhodesia where the
ordered ranks of fully uniformed men and women soldiers,
under the leadership of their own officers, can stretch on either
side of the saluting base as far as the eye can see, or the Ascen-
sion Day morning march along the Bahnhofstrasse in Zurich,
or the colourful weekday evening congress march at Skansen
in Stockholm. These—and the many like them—are superb
occasions of public Christian witness and long may they

continue, but the outdoor witness of local Salvationists in their local setting is a sight for which praise should continually be given.

I last visited Scarborough on one of the hottest weekends of the 1975 summer. The officers and soldiers of that corps began their first open-air of the day at ten o'clock in the morning, and there were also three separate indoor meetings. But at a quarter to eight in the evening the corps emerged from the citadel in Alma Parade, the band playing and the soldiers marching as cheerfully as if it had been that hour in the morning—along the Valley Bridge Road, by Somerset Terrace and then down Vernon Road to the Foreshore, preceded by their flags—six of them all told, the senior corps flag, the senior band flag, the songster flag, the young people's corps flag and the corps cadet flag—riding high in the breeze over the heads of the holiday makers who parted to allow the march to go through. To adapt Cromwell slightly, I thanked God for the Salvationist who knows what he fights for and loves what he knows.

This is one of the Army's principal strengths. The soldier— i.e. the laity—is as committed as the officer. He is not just a member, content to attend one service on a Sunday. Some time ago a leader in *The Church Times* was pleading that laymen— 'miners, transport workers, electricians, insurance agents, factory workers'—be given a place in the life of the church. 'Many of these [continued the comment] have received no continuous education since leaving school. They are material in the rough, but among them are men of great devotion and force of character . . . and are the stuff which has made the backbone of The Salvation Army.' With the proviso that the range of our people is considerably wider than that leader writer supposed, between 1963 and 1969 I was given abundant proof of his assertion.

For example, an invitation reached me from the Principal at Bretton Hall, a teacher training college specialising in the arts, to address the student body. I was unaware even of the exact location of the college but on the principle that if an invitation could be accepted, it should be, I went—to be

E

courteously received and, at the conclusion of my talk and the subsequent discussion, to be asked to participate in the mid-week assembly the following morning. Then I understood why I was there. Four of the students who were Salvationists had been appointed to lead the gathering and wished me to share this responsibility with them. I was, of course, in full uniform, but this did not embarrass them in any way. Before I left the Principal gently chided me that, on a Sunday morning, my faithful four would put themselves to no small inconvenience to visit the nearest Army corps instead of remaining for the voluntary college service. 'Do not ask me to rebuke them', I replied. 'We Salvationists are incorrigibly fond of the Army!'

A like experience befell me the following year at Cambridge where undergraduates who were members of our Students' Fellowship asked me to address an open meeting at Emmanuel on 'the role of The Salvation Army in contemporary society'— with discussion to follow. There can be a certain arrogance in the atmosphere of what has been called 'the condescending universities of Oxford and Cambridge', but this did not deter my fellow Salvationists from acknowledging whose they were and whom they served.

This total identification can be seen in the older generation as well as the younger. In my last year of office the headmaster of the Talbot County Combined School, himself a local officer in a south country corps, invited me to share in the dedication of his new school buildings. I walked through the brand-new class rooms and untrodden playing fields of which he was justifiably proud, and then joined in the meeting of thanksgiving which was attended by the staff, the pupils, their parents, the neighbouring clergy and ministers as well as representatives of the local council. 'This is my parish,' said the head to me before I left. There was no hiding of his light under any bushel. As John Boyd, a local officer in our Catford corps, observed after his election as general secretary of the A.E.U.W.: 'Everyone knows where I stand in the things that matter most.'

In like manner I see in our officers the same total involvement in the service of God and the Army.

More than five hundred miles west of the Queensland coast-line and nearly a thousand north-west of Brisbane lies the mining community of Mount Isa. Our cause there had never been over strong and certainly the condition of our properties left much to be desired. But the mines administration let it be known that they would provide the materials for a new corps hall if we would provide the labour. Happily there was an older man with some building experience who had responded to the call of officership and he, with a younger comrade, was appointed to this town of torrid temperatures. In due course the work began, and one afternoon one of the leading mining officials paid an unannounced call to see how it was progressing. He saw no one on site except two men, stripped to the waist, so busily pouring concrete that they failed to notice him. 'Is your officer around?' the visitor called out. The older man straightened his sunburnt back and spoke for them both. 'We are the officers,' he replied. This was a dedication to work for which no provision—to my knowledge—has ever been made in our rule book.

There can be an equally complete dedication to people which also goes beyond the call of duty.

In a gathering of officers in Lahore the meeting programme indicated that three western officers were to sing. The number of expatriates present on that occasion could be counted on the fingers of both hands; the rest of the group of several hundreds were nationals. I asked the three men—one Canadian, two British—to the platform, and a hush spread over the meeting as it was realised that they were singing some verses of Christian devotion—in Urdu. By the end of the first verse all was still; at the close of the last there was silence as the singers resumed their seats—and then prolonged applause broke out all over the hall. The Pakistani officers were spontaneously acknowledging this public sign of identification with them.

A parallel experience occurred in a similar meeting in Seoul. Any reader familiar with Korean practice will know that shoes must be removed before coming on to an Army platform. The only concession to this custom is to provide western visitors—such as ourselves—with something akin to an overshoe. Two American officers with their wives were to present a mixed quartet. The husband of one couple was the chief medical officer at our Army hospital; the other was on the headquarters staff. They must have loosened their shoes in anticipation for, even as I was resuming my seat after having called upon them, they were on the platform in their stockinged feet and had begun to sing in Korean: 'Jesus, keep me near the Cross'. 'Near the Cross'!—those four people were, though they would be the last to say so. No international movement can hope to escape the racial tensions of the age in which it is working, but if in any degree these are transcended in the Army it is because at the ground floor level the expatriate officer is accepted by the national because he himself is accepted by the expatriate.

This truth is the legal offspring of the honoured evangelical phrase—'the passion for souls'. The actual words may be used somewhat less than formerly. We are a shade more reticent about announcing what is our supreme passion, but that officers are still so motivated is beyond question. I can yet see the wife of a General Secretary who had given the greater part of her life to service in lands other than her own, kneeling unselfconsciously at the Mercy Seat at the conclusion of an officers' meeting. Had I employed even the gentlest of language to hint that she, of all people, needed no further seal upon her years of dedication, she might well have replied: 'Suffer it to be so.' Even the sacred fire needs refuelling.

Coming down the public stairway of an overseas head-quarters I turned a corner to discover an officer kneeling in prayer with a middle-aged man. They were complete strangers but, seeing the Army uniform the man had spoken of his heart's unease—whereupon his new-found friend knelt down with him on the stone landing, ignoring the human traffic moving both up and down.

Seated in a modest council house quarters waiting for the return of the young married Captain who was both running the corps and studying for his Ph.D. at the nearby university, the door opened and in he came—supporting a youngish woman who fell into, rather than sat down in, the only armchair in the room. She was very much the worse for wear. Her clothing was wet and soiled where she had fallen into the muddy puddles in the street. Passing in his jalopy, the officer had noticed her plight and had brought her in out of the rain. To my embarrassment she started to cling to me but I dared not set her down lest she think herself unwanted. In her intoxicated condition hot coffee was of much more value than any curtain lecture and, when finally her address was discovered the concern that had picked her up took her home.

When some mournful spirit confides in me that the Army is not what it once was, I think of our officer corps—and agree. There is a difference. An officer does not belong to what William Booth once called 'the dangerous classes' because he has had a formal education. We are learning that there is no just cause or impediment why a brilliant intellect may not be wedded to a compassionate heart. It is in this happy marriage that lies the ever-increasing usefulness of my fellow officers. I will hear no word against the scholar. If God has no need of our brains He has less use for our ignorance.

It is true that theological fashions change. Yesterday's daring speculation is tomorrow's old hat. It is therefore not surprising that some of the faithful are bewildered and jump to the unjustified conclusion that theology should be treated as Henry Ford treated history—as bunk. But the genuine scholar is devout of heart and charitable in his judgments. If—in the words of John XXIII—I pray God to 'preserve me from underestimating study, I must beware of attaching to it an exaggerated and absolute value. Study is one eye, the left eye; if the right one is missing, what is the use of a single eye?' Or, for that matter, of one leg? A man needs both to walk.

This, with variations according to congregation and setting, has been my theme in officers' meetings both large and small. These have ranged from the handful gathered in the living-room of the officers' quarters in La Paz to the hundreds filling the Centennial Temple in New York. But whether few or many in numbers, each has been a homogeneous company. That is to say, all are men and women who have embraced the same vocation. None is there except in obedience to an initial divine compulsion. None is there for commercial reasons, for commercial rewards—save for a modest security—are non-existent. Whatever their varied cultural backgrounds, none is there but who is convinced of the uniqueness of the revelation of God in the historic Jesus of Nazareth and of the consequent ethical demands of this revelation upon man, which demands can be met only in the strength of Him who requires them. Most importantly, all who are present are of one mind that he who preaches this gospel must himself be an example of it, which is why the Salvation Army officer is literally 'servant of all'. This does not mean that he has a 'skivvy' mentality with no mind for anything but life's most menial tasks. If he takes upon himself the service of the lowest, it is because he is possessed by the spirit of the highest—the mind of Christ Himself. Such are the salt of any movement—which is why it is true to say that the Army will rise or fall with its officer corps.

They themselves are fully aware that the redemption of the world will call for that quality of caring which will exclude no man nor be abashed by any setting in which he may be found. Not being illiterate, they know of the confident claim in certain quarters that man can work out his own salvation. Is there anything impossible to a being who has set foot upon the moon and who is currently exploring the recesses of space? Might he not finally usurp the place of God and create life itself? Whatever the answer to that question, it is certain that he could never create that unwearying concern which is known as redeeming love. That is solely and wholly a divine work. The love which alone can heal man's self-inflicted wounds is the love of God shed abroad in the human heart by His Spirit. It is not the work of man. It is the gift of God.

12

The Reason of Things

CERTAIN QUESTIONS ABOUT the Army recur like hardy annuals and, so long as they are asked—or implied, so long must they be answered even though they may have been dealt with many times before.

For example, in a brief but generous review of *No Discharge in this War*, the *Expository Times* referred to the Army's 'deviations from orthodoxy but not from the gospel.' We can be well content that we do not deviate from the gospel, but what is this 'orthodoxy' from which we are supposed to have departed? Is not the word one of the most subjective in the whole religious vocabulary? As William Warburton said to Lord Sandwich: 'Orthodoxy is my doxy; heterodoxy is another man's orthodoxy.' Would it be over-simplistic to argue that loyalty to the gospel relieves us of any obligations to concern ourselves with this abstraction—orthodoxy? But it could be that the reviewer sees our deviation in terms of our quasi-military structure and terminology, our practice of the equality of the sexes in the service of God, and our faith that the grace of God is freely offered and can be fully received without the employment of any material elements or the use of a particular form of words. On these points we are unrepentant. From my experience I do not see the Army departing from its time-honoured position, nor would it profit us as a Movement, nor the work of God in general, to do so. But we are always willing to give a reason for the convictions we cherish.

So far as our administrative structures are concerned,

William Booth did not set out with purpose aforethought to
create 'The Salvation Army'. It is well known that he had been
a superintendent minister in the Methodist New Connexion
from which he resigned because the Liverpool Conference of
1861 was unwilling to release him from circuit work so that
he could devote himself to full-time evangelism. It would be
fruitless at this time of day to try to allocate responsibility
for this rift. Enough that both William and Catherine forsook
the security which was theirs in obedience to what they believed
to be the leading of God. Some four years of itinerant evangelism followed until, in the summer of 1865, William Booth
was passing a religious service which was being held outside
'The Blind Beggar'—a public house on the Whitechapel
Road—when the leader invited any Christian friend desiring
to take part to do so. William responded and, as he said himself, found his destiny.

This mission had several names, beginning with The
Christian Revival Association and ending up as The Christian
Mission. But even before the historic three-man early morning
consultation in William Booth's bedroom approving the
annual report for 1878 in which the two words 'salvation
army' replaced 'volunteer army' as a description of the nature
and work of the mission, the winds of change had already
begun to blow. For example, two years previously Railton
had completed his own personal study of the religious condition of the country. This was on sale before the end of 1877
and the title page read:

HEATHEN ENGLAND

Being a description of the utterly godless condition of the vast majority of the
English nation, and the establishment,
growth, system and success of

AN ARMY FOR ITS SALVATION

consisting of working people
under the generalship of

WILLIAM BOOTH

There was an instant case for reducing the cumbrous title of 'General Superintendent of The Christian Mission' to 'General'. At Whitby a poster to this effect was issued by Cadman to announce a visit from his leader. Railton had already begun to sign himself as: 'Your ever-to-be-faithful Lieutenant'. In retrospect it is clear that these—and all other kindred spirits—acted more wisely than they knew.

No word is more biblical both in its root and content than salvation for it encompasses the whole sweep of God's redeeming power, both for unregenerate man and the society which he has made. And could the good fight of faith be waged without soldiers? There was no need to look beyond the pages of the New Testament for a militant vocabulary. If Charles Wesley could bid his 'Soldiers of Christ, arise', and Robert Browning apostrophise his soldier-saints, and Charles Haddon Spurgeon announce from where the Lord drew his best soldiers, then William Booth must not be denied his officers, soldiers and recruits. What is more to the point, his soldiers did not just exist as a figure of speech in a line of poetry. They were flesh and blood beings forming a disciplined Christian body. The holy war was the one that mattered and these soldiers were for real.

Now if it be asked where is the place of what Adolf Harnack called this 'militia Christi', the answer is as an integral part of the people of God. And as for our right so to be accepted, we offer ourselves to the most searching test of all—which is not the rite of initiation by baptism (though we seek as God shall help us to bring up our children in the fear and admonition of the Lord), nor of participation in any sacrament (though we do not doubt for one moment that any approach made in faith by a believer to the throne of grace is rewarded), nor by the acceptance of a particular administrative structure (though we gladly recognise that it pleases God to use His several servants whether they be called Pastor or Father or Reverend, and whether hands have been laid upon them or not)—but of whether or not we possess the spirit of Christ. This is the one essential test. 'If a man does not possess the spirit of Christ, he is no Christian.' But he who bears the fruit of the Spirit belongs to the True Vine, for that fruit has no other source.

Far from there being a fixed pattern of 'orthodoxy' to which every individual or group must conform, the people of God manifest a happy diversity in unity and a happy unity in diversity. Lest it be thought I am speaking above my station, the phrase is owed to the Lady Margaret Professor of Divinity at the University of Oxford. The claim that one particular church, and that church alone, is the one true church, is not seriously argued by serious scholars nowadays. We are all brethren, even though some of us may be more separated than others. Organic union—meaning a unity of theology, of structure, of authority and of worship—while desirable, even obligatory, in some eyes, cannot be biblically justified. Apart from the 'High Priest of our profession' and the people of God in general who are 'a royal priesthood', there are no priests save those of Judaism in the New Testament. The mother church at Jerusalem gave her rulings, reached after open discussion, but as that sturdy Anglican, H. M. Gwatkin, wrote: 'The unity they acknowledged was still essentially spiritual . . . Unity of government or order there was not yet. Every church was independent of the rest and free to serve Christ in its own way, if only it did serve Christ.'

Nor can organic union be deduced from what we know of the mind of Christ. He did pray for His disciples 'that they may be one', but His prayer had nothing to do with what are sometimes unhappily described as ecclesiastical mergers. The kind of unity of which He was thinking is pictured in the phrase: 'even as we are one'. This is the unity of the Father and the Son and, as Jesus had already spoken of the Spirit who would come and who would be to the disciples what He had been in the days of His flesh, we may reasonably suppose that He had in mind the rich diversity of the Trinity. This far transcends our finite powers of comprehension but is surely a unity whose diversity is infinite.

These things being so, ought we not to cease to exclude this or that group of believers from the people of God (which is also the body of Christ) on the ground that their ministry is defective—i.e. it does not correspond with our own, or their sacramental practices are irregular—i.e. they are not in harmony with ours, or they lack an unbroken tactile succession—i.e. they cannot present a continuous ecclesiastical pedigree dating back to Pentecost. To persist with such demands is virtually to argue that the Holy Spirit, instead of leading men into all truth, has had no new thing either to do or to say, whereas no man can call Jesus Lord—either in the first or the twentieth century—save by the Spirit. If this be so, then all who furnish that sign infallible are incontestably His. In this year of grace no one will have the effrontery to tell the Lord whom He may recognise as His own and whom He may not.

Similarly, and with the greatest respect for our elder brethren, we would bear our testimony to the truth that the unsearchable riches of Christ are available to all who approach the throne of grace in faith. If it is by grace that we are saved through faith, by that same means we may grow in the knowledge of our Lord and Saviour Jesus Christ. In other words, we believe in and personally experience the spiritual realities which the sacraments are declared to mediate.

This does not mean that we are 'against' the sacraments. We are not. William Booth made this clear in an interview with Sir Henry Lunn which appeared in *The Review of the Churches* as far back as April, 1895. We have never been so foolish as to deny that there are Christian ceremonies which, though not practised by ourselves, are a means of grace to the believer who observes them in faith. All we are saying— and then only to the praise of God and Him alone—is that in our meetings for worship, in our private devotions and in our public activities, we enjoy the same immediate presence of the risen Lord as do other believers when the Host is elevated or the bread and wine received. The Salvationist believes in the Real Presence as ardently as any churchman.

Indeed, it would be impossible to engage in some of the activities undertaken by a Salvationist—for example, witnessing in a downtown street meeting or helping a beaten man in a social service centre—without the blessing of Him whose mercy extends to all. Such occasions make faith in the Real

Presence not less but more essential, for if those about His work at His bidding cannot know the immediacy of their living Lord at all times, who can declare Him to be present at any specified time ? The truth is that 'Here is Thy footstool, and there rest Thy feet where live the poorest, the lowliest and the lost.'

Our non-observance of the traditional sacraments is not the fruit of any theological carelessness, nor of some slap-happy evangelism which thinks it to be of no consequence whether these have any place in our corporate life or not. On the contrary, this matter is of the utmost importance, and that is why the Salvationist prefers (to use the Quaker Barclay's phrase) 'the power to the form, the substance to the shadow.' The communion he desires is to feed on Him who called Himself 'the bread of life.' This is the one thing needful whatever the material aids, or absence of such aids, by which the divine nourishment is received. What matters is the food, not the table or paten on which it is served. This reasoning may be unacceptable to some—perhaps to many, but it would be an amazing leap forward in genuine ecumenism if all the churches would but acknowledge the presence of their sovereign Lord wherever He is pleased to be present—which is, of course, wherever the faithful gather in His name— and whatever the means whereby His grace is received. This is not—repeat not—being urged on behalf of The Salvation Army, but because in this way the church at large would be strengthened by a new realisation of the breadth of her borders and the richness of her corporate life, as rich as humanity itself. To fail to do this is sadly to fall into the ancient error of limiting the Holy One. Whom God is pleased to bless man is powerless to excommunicate.

It is recognised that there are very many who hold most firmly that certain sacraments are of divine institution, and yet it has to be remembered that since the days of Westcott and Hort there has been wide agreement that Luke 22:19(b) is an interpolation. The New English Bible relegates the words of institution to a footnote. This means that while each of the Gospels record the event which is called the last (or the Lord's) supper, no Gospel records any command to observe this particular meal as a perpetual memorial to the self-offering of Jesus for us men and for our salvation. Nor is there any suggestion in the Acts of the Apostles that the Early Church—either at Pentecost or subsequently—established a special communion meal, that is to say if the distinction between the love-feast and the Eucharist is maintained. What is said is that 'breaking bread in private houses believers shared their meals with unaffected joy.'

The only other New Testament reference to the common meal is in I Corinthians 11:23-26—and then seemingly because of the abuses which had crept in. 'Your meetings [said the Apostle] tend to do more harm than good.' May it not further be asked—and this without giving offence to any—whether this single passage is not too slight a foundation on which to erect the (in some instances, elaborate) ritual which has arisen out of the simple act of remembering the Lord Jesus when sharing food and drink in any convenient private dwelling? Let me add that the question is not raised in any polemical spirit. I am not seeking to persuade anyone to share my views. But is not our Lord's intention more perfectly fulfilled in following His example than in sharing a rite which it is not certain He required and which, in addition, has given rise possibly to more disagreements than any other matter in church life? As General Orsborn wrote and as Salvationists frequently sing:

> My life must be Christ's broken bread,
>   My love His outpoured wine,
> A cup o'erfilled, a table spread
>   Beneath His name and sign,
> That other souls, refreshed and fed,
>   May share His life through mine.

I might again be charged with error if I said that the position of women in the ministry is less disputatious. So far as the Army is concerned the recognition of women as ministers of God has not been in contention since Whit Sunday, 1860,

when Mrs. William Booth confessed her disobedience to the
Lord's leadings in the morning meeting and preached on 'Be
filled with the Spirit' at night. In the providence of God it
was an invitation to her to conduct an evangelistic campaign
in Rotherhithe in March, 1865, which brought her husband
to settle with the family in London and so led to the decisive
encounter outside 'The Blind Beggar'. By the time of the
change of name in 1878 nearly half of the officer strength of
the newly named Army were women and they were in charge
of two out of every five corps.

Yet their presence was resented by an influential section
of the religious world of that day. 'How can any real good
(asked the *Church Times* on November 25th, 1881) be expected
of a Movement which systematically takes the opposite line
to St. Paul's injunction that women should keep silence in the
churches?' But Mrs. Booth's faith did not fail. She dared to
prophesy that 'whether the church will allow women to speak
in its assemblies can only be a matter of time'—and time has
vindicated her judgment. The recent verdict of the Anglican
Communion in this country that there is no fundamental
objection to the ordination of women is a most welcome sign.
The full implementation of that judgment may take time, but
the rising tide will clear the beach of any theological Canutes.
It can be taken for granted that the Army will never abandon
the principle that a woman officer, equally with a man, may
serve as a minister of the gospel. We already owe too much to
our women officers, both single and married, to disobey the
light from heaven which shone round about Catherine Booth
as she sat in her pew in the Bethesda chapel. After more than a
century the splendour of that moment continues to illuminate
the life of many an African and Asian woman officer, revealing
still wider fields of service in which she may exercise those
gifts which God has given her. If this be yet another of those
deplorable deviations from orthodoxy, pray God there may
yet be many more.

13

Not Unto Us, O Lord

THE CENTENARY WAS a high-water mark in the life of the Army, an event which captured the imagination of officers and soldiers throughout the world. All roads led to London in the summer of 1965. There were some two thousand official delegates drawn from all five continents, but many times that number of Salvationists—particularly local officers and soldiers —came from many countries at their own charge in order to join in this event of a lifetime. The self-supporting territories in the Army world gave generously so that as many delegates as possible from Africa and Asia might share in these celebrations. One happy result of this arrangement was the presence of the Léopoldville (now Kinshasa) Central Hall Band. That a ten days' programme, sometimes with five public meetings in a single day held in such separate buildings as the Royal Albert Hall, the Westminster Central Hall, the former Clapton Congress Hall and the Regent Hall, was carried through without any breakdowns was in no small measure due to the skill of the main planning council under the chairmanship of Commissioner Arthur Pallant, the unwearying oversight of the chief executive secretary, Colonel Frederick Kiff, and the diligence with which each Salvationist on duty carried out his allotted duty.

One of the questions addressed to nominees at the 1963 High Council was: 'Will you without delay press forward with plans for the observance of the hundredth anniversary

of The Salvation Army in 1965 ?' There was only one answer
to that—and one early result was that I was asked to call on
Sir Michael Adeane at Buckingham Palace on the morning
of Thursday, March 28th, 1964, to discuss our request that the
Queen might grace the inaugural meeting of the Centenary
on the afternoon of Thursday, June 25th, 1965. From that
moment the furtherance of our plans was aided and abetted
by all whose help we sought.

In one sense it is not difficult to ensure that public buildings
are well filled for Salvation Army rallies. Our people love to
assemble themselves together, and years of practice have
given the administration a command of the necessary know-
how. Every leader in turn—not least myself—has reason to be
grateful for this expertise. But the thirty principal meetings
in this country of these international rejoicings were not
intended to be a haphazard string of varied events, each
without doubt possessing its own interest but none related to
its neighbour. It would be tiresome at this time of day to give
an itemised account of each gathering. Enough to say that
the whole period was designed to be a demonstration of the
continuing spiritual life of that part of the universal church of
God known as The Salvation Army, with particular reference
to our principles and practices. Under God this would be a
confirmation to Salvationists everywhere of their own faith, as
well as a public witness to the truth that we who in time past
were not a people were now a people of God to show forth the
praise of Him who had called us out of darkness into His
marvellous light.

It is true that one religious leader used the occasion to
enquire whether the time had not come 'for the disbandment
of this regiment of the army of the Lord so that its spirit and
its experience might be regrouped in one great reunited church
for the battles of tomorrow ?' This flattering but too facile
metaphor notwithstanding, the spirit of a regiment is not
shared by laying up its colours—at least not when it still
possesses arms and equipment and personnel with the will and
heart to go on fighting. As well ask Wellington why he did not
disband his Guards in the middle of the Peninsular War.

Not that we claim any seniority in the Lord's host. We are possibly the youngest of that company and this—among other reasons—is why the spirit of the Centenary was expressed in General Orsborn's lines:

Not unto us, O Lord,
    But unto Thy great name
Our trumpets are awake,
    Our banners are aflame.
We boast no battle ever won;
The victory is Thine alone.

We were that foolish thing,
    Unversed in worldly ways,
Which Thou didst choose and use
    Unto Thy greater praise.
Called and commissioned from afar
To bring to naught the things that are.

One welcome suggestion was that the memory of William Booth should be nationally honoured by an acknowledgment of him in Westminster Abbey, and I shall forever be grateful to Dr. E. S. Abbott for the sympathetic way in which he received this proposal. Indeed it was the Dean and Chapter who decided that the bust of the Founder should be placed in the St. George's Chapel where his senior active officer-grandson, Commissioner W. Wycliffe Booth, shared in the unveiling on the afternoon of Friday, July 2nd, 1965.

It was in keeping with the Army's friendly relationship with the historic churches—we have been a member of the World Council of Churches since its inception in 1948—that the Archbishop of Canterbury, Dr. Michael Ramsey, the Archbishop of Westminster, Cardinal John Heenan, and the Moderator of the Free Church Federal Council, the Rev. Peter McCall, should appear on the platform at the Royal Albert Hall on either side of Her Majesty the Queen. This was the occasion when the Anglican Archbishop remarked that he had never seen 'a gloomy member of The Salvation

Army'. His Grace may not have been aware that another distinguished Anglican had earlier said much the same. Dean Inge once confessed that though he knew little about the Army, when he was at St. Paul's he used to see many Salvationists in the area and 'they all seemed very happy.'

Nor was the State slow to acknowledge the contribution made by the Army to the well-being of the nation. As the Home Secretary, Sir Frank Soskice, said when referring to the deliberate hostility of the eighties: 'Now you no longer need our protection, but my colleagues and I need your help as much as ever before.' And just as on six of the Centenary weeknights a separate evangelistic meeting was held in the Regent Hall (close by Oxford Circus) in order to emphasise that our primary concern is with the preaching of the gospel, so one of the peak moments in this crowded inaugural meeting was when, to the subdued accompaniment of the five hundred voice chorus, a songster soloist sang:

> O save me, dear Lord,
>   I plead by Thy mercy
> O save me, dear Lord.

It was left to *The War Cry* to describe how 'a meeting festooned with applause fell into silence.' Because the work of the Army's caring services had been acknowledged barely fifteen minutes earlier, it was impossible to dismiss that prayer as a deplorable exhibition of a spiritual selfishness which was concerned with one's own salvation. It is the most ardent social reformer who knows from experience how often his best-laid schemes for the general good of mankind founder on the jagged and merciless rocks of self-interest. As Laurens van der Post has written: 'The only sure way to rid life of villains is first to rid ourselves of the villain within.'

This is why social caring can never be separated from personal evangelism. Make the tree good, said Jesus; good fruit will then follow. It is a vain dream to suppose that the kingdom of God will come on earth without the cleansing power of the grace of God. Even a secular utopia cannot

run on the crude oil of personal selfishness. We know what
tensions can sometimes arise within the general body of
Christian believers where the reconciling power of God is
presumed to have done its blessed work. How then can we
hope to persuade men to live in good fellowship where this
over-riding motive is absent? 'Kingdom of Christ, for thy
coming we pray.' The operative words—'of Christ'. Christian
evangelism is neither the preaching by itself of the first of
Christ's two great commandments, nor yet the second. These
two requirements, joined by Jesus, may not be put asunder
by man. The full gospel—a phrase beloved in certain quarters—
includes both. The first commandment issues in a barren
piety unless the second be obeyed. But the second remains
impossible of accomplishment without the first.

Nor is Christian evangelism only the presentation of intellectual answers to the intellectual problems of questioning minds.
This is undoubtedly part of the work of evangelism. We must
be ready with a reason for the hope which we invite them to
embrace. But a man has to do more than mentally assent to
the truths of the Christian faith. The will must bow to Him
who is the Author of that faith.

Yet again, evangelism is more than an appeal to those who
have a fringe interest in the church—men and women whose
names are on a roll but whose allegiance may not rise to more
than a solitary annual attendance. The work of evangelism is
too difficult to sit in judgment upon any effort, but it is clear
that a proportion of the 'converts' in some well-publicised
campaigns of our day already have some church affiliation—
even though it be nominal. Of course, if the faith of any such
is rekindled, all praise to God. But do not let us suppose that
their quickening makes any serious diminution of the terrifying
total of those who, at all levels of our western society, do not
acknowledge even the shadow of any such affiliation. Any
Christian evangelism worthy of the name must accept the
mind-wearying, heart-breaking, soul-consuming task of offering the gospel to those who are totally indifferent to that gospel
because they are totally convinced that it is an optional extra
which they can decline without loss. Some are even under the

illusion that they are better off without it. This is not a seller's
market for the would-be evangelist. He is offering wares which
àre not universally desired. Nowadays it is the sinner who is
often so certain that he has no need of repentance.

This is why the Centenary also sought to demonstrate our
unalterable conviction that, whatever the cost and whatever
the disappointments, the gospel must still be taken by the
people to the people where the people are. The report compiled by William Booth in May, 1878, to which reference was
made in the previous chapter, carried a quotation from A. C.
Tait (Archbishop of Canterbury, 1868–1882) calling upon the
Church 'to arm, as far as we can, the whole population in the
cause of Jesus Christ.' To which the answer must surely be:
'How shall they believe in Him of whom they have not heard?'
With good cause, therefore, the Centenary began and ended
with a weekday open-air—the first in the Whitechapel Road
where William Booth began; the econd on the final Saturday
of the celebrations in Trafalgar Square. On this occasion the
march moved from the Horse Guards Parade, past St. James's
Palace, Westminster Abbey and the Houses of Parliament—
symbols of Court, Church and People—to the Square where
the throngs of listeners overflowed on to the balconies of the
National Gallery. From the plinth of Nelson's column the
entire square was an unbroken sea of faces. The Army was
witnessing in strength in the same fashion in which it began
that the Christian gospel is for all men in all places at all times.

A corollary is that hand in hand with the preaching of the
gospel goes personal witness to the power of the gospel. In
some quarters the worth of Christian testimony is ignored;
in others it is derided, and not only by Shaw's ridicule of the
character he himself created—Snobby ('Wot prawce selvytion
nah?') Price, but by some men of the cloth who decry it as
well. A recent book on preachers and preaching castigated the
practice of getting 'someone well-known to the public . . .
to give his testimony. This is deemed to be of much greater
value that the preaching and exposition of the gospel . . . I
put all this under the heading of entertainment.'

But what is a messenger of the gospel doing to refuse a place to a witness to the power of that gospel? There is no need to flinch from the word entertainment. Entertain me in your home —and you provide me with rest and refreshment. My hunger is appeased; my bodily weariness vanishes; my mind revives in your company. Before I leave I thank you for your entertainment. According to Hebrews 13:2 you have wrought a good work. Now if the outcome of personal testimony is that desire is reborn and faith is renewed in some faltering heart—that is to say, this is a God-blessed means of spiritual renewal—why should there be a question mark against testimony? Must we cripple ourselves by fighting with one hand deliberately tied behind our own back?

Addressing the Yearly Meeting of the Society of Friends in July, 1882, Mrs. Booth quoted her husband as saying that 'the people do not come so much to hear the preacher as to look at the Bills and Dicks . . . who have been converted, and still more to hear them speak.' This is to tilt the balance somewhat in the opposite direction but at least the preacher is not forbidden to preach.

The Centenary saw these two forces join hands for in all the principal meetings—out of doors and in—word and witness were united. The criterion was not, is this man well known but, does he know Jesus as Saviour and Lord? A short list of Salvationists who testified during those ten days as to what great things the Lord had done for them included an Antarctic explorer, a Norwegian nurse, a Pakistani officer, a wartime German glider pilot, a Kenyan student, a British housewife, a Swedish broadcaster, a South African doctor, a folk school administrator—and space would fail me to tell of the rest.

Last of all, this gathering from the four corners of the earth made it plain that 'in this new life, nationality, or race, or education, or social position, is unimportant' (Colossians 3:11). Those taking part in the final open-air included a married woman officer from the Netherlands, an African local officer from Harare, a single woman officer from Japan and a Canadian man officer. This fact—along with the allied truth that 'gone is the distinction between . . . male and female' was made even plainer, if that were possible, in the Westminster Abbey service. The colour party which accompanied the Army flag to the steps of the sanctuary was made up of twelve men and twelve women ranging from a Finnish Master of Arts to a Maori woman Salvationist and, in addition to representatives from the western world, included officers and soldiers from the Caribbean and Korea, from Brazil and India, from Ghana and Indonesia, from the Congo and Hong Kong. As plainly as flesh and blood could say it, that significant procession was declaring that whatever the national policy of this government or that, or whatever the personal prejudice which might still rule some unenlightened hearts and minds, this Movement held every man to be equally dear to God because in Christ He died for all.

In his last coherent conversation with his eldest son, Bramwell, William Booth said: 'I have been thinking again of the world as a whole. I have been thinking of all nations and peoples as one family.' This is how the Salvationist continues to think of the world. It is the only Christian way in which to think of the world. Anything other than this does despite to the truth that 'God so loved the world'.

Over the years there have been many encounters with the media—by far most of them on a friendly basis, but from the Centenary onwards one of the oft repeated suggestions was that this piece of Victoriana known as The Salvation Army was surely on its way out. Was it not one with the bustle and the hansom cab—a quaint nineteenth-century survival whose day was virtually done?

One became almost grateful for a ball repeatedly pitched so short that even a batsman like myself in the Sunday-school league was given a chance to hit it over the sight screen. The question misjudges both the nature of man and the nature of our society. The fact that a man may not consciously desire a Saviour is no proof that he does not need one. Discount the biblical word that man does not live by bread alone, we are still left with R. H. Tawney's description of him as 'that timid staring creature so compounded as to require not only money, but light and air and water, not to mention such non-economic goods as tranquillity, beauty and affection'. So long as the soul of man thirsts—be it never so faintly—for a drink divine, so long will there be needed those who know where the fountains of living water are to be found.

As for the nature of our society, as long as there are broken homes and chronic alcoholics, compulsive gamblers and panders who prey upon human weaknesses, children who are socially deprived and adults who are socially inadequate, rebellious adolescents and lonely pensioners, the young who at heart fear life and the old who are afraid of death, so long will there be needed men and women who are willing to pay the price of caring. In face of these incontrovertible facts let no one anticipate, much less welcome, the demise of any compassionate community. There are none too many of them as it is and, to put it mildly, The Salvation Army might be missed. For my part, I am well content to soldier on in this Christian regiment because here there is no continuing city. We seek one whose builder and maker is God.

Index

oh

S

St. Albans, 106
St. Helens, 8
St. Helier, 47
Sampson, Lily, 85
Sangster, William, 118
Scarborough, 129
Scotney, Hubert, 89
Scott, Mary, 55
Sedding, Frederick, 18
Segawa, Yasowo, 111
Selbie, W. B., 116
Sheppard, Dick, 118
Slim, William, 81
Smartt, Herb, 92
Smith, Albert, 91
Smith, C. Ryder, 49
Soper, Lord, 118
Soskice, Frank, 146
Stacey, Nicholas, 113
Street, 7
Swinfen, J. H., 107

T

Trowbridge, 7

W

Walker, Alan, 120
Walz, Arthur, 91
Warren, Henry, J., 82, 104
Warren, Max, 45,
Warrington, 8, 12, 33
Webb, Joy, 108
Westcott, Herbert, 107
Westminster Abbey, 145
Whatmore, Hugh, 27
Whitehead, A. N., 45
Whyte, Alexander, 45
Wickberg, Erik, 77, 107
Wood, H. G., 117
Woodward, Leonard, 73, 77

Y

Yeovil, 7
Young, Dinsdale, 116